VOICES

FROM LEIMERT PARK

A POETRY ANTHOLOGY

TSEHAI
Publishers & Distributors

ဗာ www.tsehaipublishers.com ಆ

VOICES

FROM LEIMERT PARK

A POETRY ANTHOLOGY

EDITED BY

SHONDA BUCHANAN

TSEHAI
Publishers & Distributors

"If you wish to follow, even at a distance, the poet's calling…you've got to come out of the measurable doing universe into the immeasurable house of being…nobody else can be alive for you; nor can you be alive for anybody else."

e. e. cummings

"I don't know why I write. But I know I could not live without writing."

Gabriel Garcia Marquez

"Do like we do; just do the best you can."

Lucille Clifton

TSEHAI
Publishers & Distributors

Voices from Leimert Park: a Poetry Anthology

Tsehai books may be purchased for educational, business, or sales promotional use. For more information, please contact our special sales department.

Tsehai Publishers
P. O. Box 1881, Hollywood, CA 90078

w w w . t s e h a i p u b l i s h e r s . c o m

info@tsehaipublishers.com

ISBN-10: 1-59907-015-4 | ISBN-13: 978-1-59907-015-5

Edited by: Shonda Buchanan | Publisher: Elias Wondimu
Cover Photography and Design by Evguenl Groisman
Layout Design by Yosef Gezahegne

First Edition, Dec. 2006

Library of Congress Catalog Card Number
A catalog record for this book is available from the Library of Congress.

British Library Cataloguing in Publication Data.
A catalogue record for this book is available from the British Library.

10 9 8 7 6 5 4 3 2 1

Printed in the United States of America

CONTENTS

DEDICATION

This book is dedicated to the artists of
Los Angeles, and to the ancestors who have crossed over, all those who
helped to make a path, a place and the space for
Los Angeles' artists of color.

Absalom, Gwedolyn Brooks, Ossie Davis, Richard Fulton, Billy Higgins,
Juno Lewis, Dr. Ligon and Mrs. Ligon, Beah Richards, Dadisi Sanyika,
Horace Tapscott, Earl Underwood, and all the unspoken others.

What ever we can do, we do, in honor of you.

ACKNOWLEDGEMENTS

First, honor to the spirit of the Chumash village that first occupied the space we know today as Leimert Park, 43rd and Degnan/Crenshaw Boulevard. Absolute homage to the publisher of this text, Elias Wondimu for recognizing, supporting and pushing this into birth. Many thanks to elders, Kamau Daáood, the first master wordsmith to carve a space for the work that leapt out of The World Stage, and Billy Higgins, master drummer watching us from on high, our elders who had the vision and the spirit-knowing to listen when called.

Thank you to my two assistants Tatiana Bryant and Shawnda Young for their help on this book. Thank you Michael Datcher for bringing the organized funk to the Stage; thank you World Stage, thank you Anansi Writers Workshop. Word up Ben Caldwell for the energy, the knowledge and visual footage out of Kaos Network. Homage to Richard Fulton, founder and owner of 5th Street Dicks, also gazing down at us with that smile. To our spirit shaper, my daughter Afiya's godfather, Dadisi Sanyika, for it all--I would never have opened if not for you and the Aquarian Spiritual Center, and his lovely daughters, Tamiza, Sebek, Neth. Thank you Absalom, Kamira and Ramika, the twin lights. Thank you Afiya, my daughter, the first World Stage baby, for listening to me through it all. To Don Muhammad, our concierge, and Corneal, our home base drummer. To our bards, Blaque Pearl/Nailah, to Neo, Jason and Massa. To all those, any one who has attended a festival, a celebration, a concert at Marla Gibbs' Vision Complex, or a home-going at Crossroads; to those who glided, walked, limped, pimped, strutted and rolled down Degnan and 43rd.

Thanks to all the other voices, the dancers and drummers of Dance Collective, to the artists, Ramses, the musicians, the chess players, the coffee, tea and hot chocolate drinkers, to Ruby, the fathers, mothers and children, the business owners, Baktajua's Seika and Chaka, to Kongo Square, to Juno and Black Note, Africa by the Yard, Museum in Black, to Strange Fruit and country Jeff Tan Watts for the crazy 4 a.m. session at the Nickel that winter night; to the patrons who paid, to the loiterers who made it look crowded. To Adwin Brown for first taking me and Afiya to the World Stage in 1991. To the players and mackstresses, the wizards, and the harmless winos and the witches, to the Sisters 7, Rhonda Mitchell, Kim Benjamin, Ruth Forman, Lisa Appleberry, Adrian Bosley, Sonja Marie; to the funky pigeons, and most of all, the park's fountain spirits, the ones that came before and will come after.

Long after.

FOREWORD

"would you wear my eyes?"

Bob Kaufman

Voices rise from the village like flowers pushing through the asphalt. Words like magic spores, mushrooms appear in fertile minds, new thoughts descend from higher realms. Medicine to counteract the forces of manipulation and coercion moving through our world like a deadly airborne virus. Bad thoughts and wrong ideas harden into oppression. Words are the cargo ships of thought and feeling, the building materials of story. Poems are the music of thought. Our stories are important. They must be told correctly. So precious are our moments here. We must remember. Learn from the journey. Flowers burst from asphalt with lips proclaiming a new day with computer at the finger tips singing.

I remember the early days in the village. It was just a few of us who put out the call. Came to this place and said this is the space we will make sacred, this is where we will ritualize and make the liberated zone. And they came: the singers, dancer the poets and musicians, the painters.

There are saints in the village. They live their lives in the community as givers, they are here with us for a time, do their work and go. Giants like Horace Tapscott, Billy Higgins, Richard Fulton, and Juno Lewis, Abasalom, the unsung, now ancestors. Many will not know these names, but the thought of them brings smiles and strength to those of us that know the story. The walls and streets are coated with our laughter and stained with our tears. Music and stories are everywhere. The poet's job is helping us to remember, showing us where the light is, what is important and sacred, what are the things worth fighting for, gather the family, lead us to the peace of understanding and self discovery, construct a world.

It is a sense of community that is being developed here in this village in these voices. This heart where we come to get the gospel, where we come to lighten our blues, laugh about our pain. Borrow a few dollars until Friday. We come looking for love and answers. We come here to place our stories at the porch of open ears. Where the young seek out their elders and are sharpened against their wisdom. The elders look to the youth for hope and strength and bathe in the glory of memory.

We remember how Marla Gibbs gave us a vision theater, we remember how Brian Breye built a Black museum as well as swept our streets. Ruby and Vanessa serving coffee and wisdom to the youth gathered at Fifth Street Dick's. We remember how Don Muhammad guarded the door to the World Stage for over a decade. We watch the artist Ramsess painting, drawing, cutting colored glass day in day out. The merchants opening their shops full of handcrafted, thoughtful items, gifts and bits of heritage, mud cloth and kente, sage and nagchampa, Djembes and shekares. Coffee beans and chai tea. Chess masters and domino divas. Scholars and panhandlers. People come, people stay, people go. The saints and the sinners. The givers and the takers. All to the back drop of an eternal drum circle. Blues on the corner, jazz at the curb and the hip hop don't stop.

Voices that live and learn here mature in their ability to tell the truth. You watch the children being born, you watch the old ones die. You witness the drama unfold. They are recorded in the voices dripping story. You take the side of truth. You tell it. You open up your chest and tell it. You tell it with strength, you shape it with care, you dress it in beauty and you approach the throne of song. You tell it, so that it has been said. You tell it hoping someone will. You say it to heal yourself. But most of all you fill yourself with poems and with reverence you tell it.

Kamau Daáood
Los Angeles, California

INTRODUCTION

The overhead light poured a bright, violating glare into the small room, casting shadows. Poet/fathers Nafis Nabawi and Anthony Lyons, and Father Amdee, a member of the Watts Prophets, sat in a circle on hard, uncomfortable chairs. Poems in hand, they ignored the chaos of the other awkwardly placed pieces of furniture pushed against the walls. It was 1991. The World Stage was a year old. Adwin Brown, my performance poetry partner, had brought my daughter Afiya and I to this space, The World Stage Performance Gallery. I looked at the men, only men, and wondered if this new cluster, the Anansi Writer's Workshop, held at a store front on Degnan Boulevard, would remain testosterone-oriented or would some sisters infiltrate and provide a balance. I didn't know that a sister, Akilah Nayo Oliver, was already one of the three founding members, she, Nafis Nabawi and Kamau Daáood. Women were already there. Anthony and Nafis both brought their wives who wrote and read poetry. Teenagers, children, and more men came to Leimert Park, to The World Stage, to comb the poetry out of their lives; to be heard. To say something.

That night, my daughter and I sat and listened. I hadn't brought any poetry to share, but what the men were saying, the tacit vulnerability, the surviving of loss and sorrow I heard in their words, a raw, complex yet basic desire to be counted as legitimate, a black man with faults and dreams, has remained as The World Stage Performance Gallery mantra: Come real or don't come at all. Or, as Michael Datcher, dynamic, suave workshop director, later labeled it, "the No Bullshit rule." Or "Read the damn poem," as Peter Harris liked to say, don't hem and haw. We don't have time for that.

Founded in 1990 by poet/activist Kamau Daáood and jazz drummer, Billy Higgins, (the most recorded jazz drummer in the world), The World Stage became a cultural icon. Although Ben Caldwell's Kaos Network opened shop in 1984 on the corner of Leimert Boulevard and 43rd, The World Stage was a beacon. Located at the bottom of an affluent black community, and sandwiched between a fast evaporating middle class black neighborhood, Leimert Park had been shunned as a blighted area, left to the homeless and drug addicts. The artists, the visionaries changed it. The energy in the space was full of the residuals of the 60s movement. Billy Higgins, a superstar by the 50s, had already broken down doors and musical barriers in New York and Los Angeles. Our mentors were old cats who'd outright defied or simply held themselves away from authority. Under their tutelage, a generation of black Los Angeles poets, painters and musicians who wrote, drew and read, played music and dominoes, and spoke ourselves into a reality that we felt, it seemed at the time, "the establishment," meant to withhold from us. The World Stage was a place for lightsound, and wordmusic, for Billy Higgins, a touchstone where he taught drum classes to local youth until his death in 2001. For Kamau Daáood, my friend and guide for the last fifteen years, it was his offering to the community, and a promise to himself as a wordsmith.

Over the next few years, Leimert Park was gradually claimed by artists, writers and dancers, Muslims and Africanists, bookworms, soothsayers and witches. The winos and homosexual prostitutes who'd previously made this area their home melded into the shadows, not disappearing, just on the outskirts, still ours. Someone has yet to write the extended history of the area as the Mecca for black artists, and before that the pillar of a real estate mogul whose family placed the Italian-like fountain askew in the actual park, and even further, hundreds of years back when this entire area was a Chumash village, and before that when it was submerged beneath water and only the spirits knew of Leimert Park's impending future. For now, I'll speak on the arrival of the poets.

An anthology like this has been a long time coming. For the last fifteen years, every place we come together, whether it was The World Stage, or someone's party, a birthday gathering, a child's naming ceremony, a funeral or a home-going, whether it was a cement corner or Fifth Street Dicks (Richard Fulton's place) backed up by a jazz band, we have always brought words. This anthology was not my idea -- we all knew it needed to happen, but we were busy living and loving, making babies and building careers. And, of course, we were writing. Yet, we knew a renaissance was happening in Los Angeles, akin to the Harlem Renaissance. But we were caught up in it, shaking, grinding our pencils down, downing endless cups of coffee at a table outside Fifth Street, trying to find the words to say it precisely the way our heart was beating the sounds out.

Consequently, the night of my 34th birthday party, my friend Elias Wondimu, founder of Tsehai Publishers, couldn't leave until he'd told me in no uncertain terms that he wanted to publish the poetry he'd heard. Elias had been on the outside looking in, he nearly wept when he heard S. Pearl Sharp and Wendy James, Peter Harris and Paul Caulderon read. When I stepped back to see what Elias saw, I realized that we were indeed a powerful and rare collective of voices. He made me promise on the threshold of my apartment that I would help him bring that energy together in a book, so that those who do not know, as Wanda Coleman says in her epilogue, that there is a chorus of West Coast black poets, fierce and gentle, honest and erotic, for those who had no clue, would know. Here it is. For the last three years, I have done my best to collect the voices.

However, when I look at the names of poets listed in this text, I see more than letters from the alphabet, I see my life, my family, our lives, spiraled in a web connecting all of the artists who made Leimert Park a permanent or transient home. So many things have been born here. I am not the only one who can testify to that. Though this text contains only a sampling of the talent, many came into a birth of sorts in Leimert Park. Kamau Daáood, also owner of now defunct Final Vinyl Collectable Records, was a product of the Watts Writers Workshop, founded after the 1965 Watts Rebellion. Billy Higgins was a Civil Rights son. One of Kamau's dearest friends, Horace Tapscott created the Pan African People's Arkestra, which fused words and music into a revolutionary high art -- the birth of an artform we have yet to see again.

Much of what has been created in Leimert Park began about rebellion and turned into a search for authenticity of artistic voice; the black/brown Los Angeles aesthetic.

This particular renaissance has been an act of defiance against those who would rather not hear what black Angelenos -- black poets, writers, musicians -- have to say. The different stages that the area has gone through, the ups and downs of the business owners, and what the neighborhood watch groups have had to deal with, are the very things that the black poet tells the world -- this mad beauty really exits.

The growth that Leimert Park has experienced reflects the lives of people, both musically, and poetically. The work that we have done and still attempt, has been touched by this kind of virulent, kinetic energy, the power of story telling, the power of the word. Our experiences have been fueled by all the movements that have come before us, Reconstruction, by Harper's Ferry, Harriet Tubman and Frederick Douglass, Toussaint L'Ouverture. Our work was, and is, inspired by Coltrane, Blakey and Sunship, by John Outterbrigde, Betty Sarr, Samella Lewis and Romare Bearden, the paintings of John Biggers and words of the Black Panther movement. Another powerful entity that added to poetic growth was Eso Won Books, one of the largest black bookstores in the country. Owners James Fugate and Tom Hamilton started their business on a cart, then opened up in three stifling rooms above Africa by the Yard, a fabric and clothe shop, on Slauson and Crenshaw. Eso Won moved again to a location in Inglewood on La Brea and Pilgrim, then to where the sotre now resides on La Brea and Coliseum. Eso Won was a catalyst for black writers and thinkers, hosting the likes of elders Dr. Yosef ben-Jochannan, Henry Clarke and Sonia Sanchez. Eso Won's mere presence was revolutionary. Along with The Aquarian Spiritual Center, a persistent burning flame of black Gnostics, Eso Won helped usher in the new movement that the poets needed; they fed us. Our recent elder, Dadisi Sanyika, fed us, told us and showed what fasting, meditation and practice could do towards transforming language into transcending actions. True Africanism.

With these aforementioned pieces as fodder, as foundation, I realized that this work is more than the poem. Being a poet is not a birthright; it is work and a responsibility. The poet's narration, the work coming out of Leimert Park was, is, the history of black and brown Los Angeles. The work we do in and around The World Stage and Fifth Street Dicks, reflects and represents the heritage and traditions, the black and brown aesthetic and language, our movement, infiltration of and access to this city. We speak the history of this city. We are the history of this California. We are its past and present; we foretold and foretell our own birth, a coming, the thriving, our flowering out into this world.

Writer e.e. cummings talks about the accountability of the poet to tell the truth the way he or she recognizes it, not as it is told to them. At the ten year reunion of the Furious Flower Conference at James Madison University in 2004, Sonia Sanchez took responsibility and called out the names of our elders and ancestors, those living and dead, who have fought the writer's battle. It was a powerful, distilling moment for those, both published and unpublished, lauded and unknown, who knew what she was doing. She was giving them back their voice; Sanchez was thanking her mentors, telling them that she, and we are continuing on with the work that they had set out for us. Yet, if we do nothing but call out into the night and serenade the moon, some like Pablo Neruda might say we've done our job as poets. Some will say we have not. And if we do nothing but tell someone who hurt us, disrespected our humanity or who loves us; tell the establishment that we know who enslaved us; we know who has bent us in unimaginable ways, Bob Kaufman, Laini Mataka will say we have done our job – for that is the poet's calling. Maybe some will say we have not.

But when a black poet from Los Angeles writes, we are tapping into everyone Sonia Sanchez named, and more. Pio Pico, and Biddy Mason are on our shoulders. More than the ancestors of Leimert Park, the Chumash, the boat people; we are calling on them all. As Sonia Sanchez did, calling upon our African ancestors, the griots, or as the Senegalese say, the gau'well, the storytellers who followed their soldiers to war with word, with song and with drum. Even closer, we are calling upon our uncle June Bug, and aunties, our cousin Jo Ann, the loud-mouth, our gangsters in the back alleys in Jordan Downs and Nickerson Gardens being beaten by police, we are calling on June Jordan, our sister Rochelle on the corner, our babies dying of AIDS in Centinela Hospital in Inglewood, our grandmothers who used to wash white women's toilet bowls in Beverly Hills, our children learning nothing about African or Mexican history in Los Angeles schools, our black politicians, our school teachers, our mothers and fathers, our friends, ourselves. We are calling. We are doing our job. Someone has to tell the story of black (and brown) Los Angeles, of Leimert Park, the other side of the "riots", the loss and love, the attempt at physical and geographical health, and the crossing over and the births of new things. We rarely indulge in wishy-washy poems that slide off your plate like a greasy egg; Leimert Park poets seldom write flimsy, flowery things that smell good in the morning, not always. We don't have time for that.

Over the years, it has become evident that the meaning of our work is inherit in the name of the place that started it all, The World Stage: We are being watched in this place that Kamau Daáood says, "is the place where we deposit our tears." We are being watched. Poets provide the waking world with a path to the inner, the ethereal, the past, and the spiritual world with a path to this one. We are a conduit for our ancestors to land here again, in our hearts, and to unfold into our words. If we, the poets, the storytellers, do not write about those tears, about the glory and loss, of our ancestors, and write ourselves, as Octavia Butler once said, into the future, no one will.

This has been a labor of love. It was important that someone take the first step towards documenting the poetic voices in an anthology format. I am grateful, and give thanks to the Creator for allowing the birth of "voices from leimert park" to come through me. Oho, Ashè.

Shonda Buchanan
Hampton, Virginia

LEIMERT PARK

my heart is a djembe drum
played upon by the dark hands
of a fifth street cappuccino
my invisible turban is an angelic saxophone solo
the sidewalk is hardened mud cloth
massaging the sole of my feet
i do West African dance steps
reflecting the sun off my Stacey Adams shoes
i stand on the o.g. corner
tell old school stories with a bebop tongue
to the hip hop future
i see new rainbows in their eyes
as we stand in puddles of melted chains

visit the black sensei
the grumpy voice
wrapped in juju
warrior spirit guarding
room full of stereotyping and ancestral story
a moor in a porkpie hat
stands with a video camera
in front of a stained glass musician
i lowride on a zebra
in front of Kongo square
we clothe ourselves in sun
and Africa by the yard
handwoven the fabric of the lives
we sculpt

there are trees in Leimert Park
under which old men do divination
with the bones of dominoes
Degnan a river, a nu Nile, on whose banks
young poets sharpen their hearts
on the polyrhythms of Billy Higgins' smile
on the world stage where Tapscott fingers

massage your collective memory
at the crossroads
a vision is shaped by a woman
who labored as a maid
and gave her wages to her village
here where children play double-dutch
with dreadlocked ropes
and believers wash the streets
with a mother's tears under kente sky
vomit up your television set
take a deep breath and exhale your fears
scrub the tombstones of those who died young
until they become mirrors
in which to see yourself
take long stares at your hands
until true love returns to your touch
then touch
stand right in a garment of light

i want to pour poems
into the open arms of your drums
i want to get in between your piano keys
and unleash the healing secrets
i want to stuff your dreams
with a bed of cleansing herbs
i want to wipe the bull's-eyes
off the backs
of your children

KAMAU DAÁOOD

VOICES FROM LEIMERT PARK:
A POETRY ANTHOLOGY

MIKAEL AHADOU

GUERRILLA POETS

Guerilla poets
Are ordinary eyes
looking out in the darkness
Looking inward
through the grates and bars
of the little hideaways
outlaws on the run
from the system.

> Guerilla poets
> fade into the background
> even as you bust them
> they evaporate into
> the concrete sidewalk
> leaving behind
> not a trace.

Guerrilla poets
are the night people
peering on lonely
street corners
standing around at 3 am as
the solitary poet zooms by.

ARMED CAMP

Armed camp
Occupation army

We must find a solution,
they say, as the barricades go up;
stop traffic! That's not oppression;
spend the night handing out citations.
We'll turn Crenshaw into a gauntlet;
Let those who dare, run the rapids;
If the motorcycles miss them
Its certain the cruisers will sink them.

Armed camp
Occupation army

Highway patrol on the one hand
and LAPD on the other;
to turn Leimert, they'd rather,
into an armed camp; if need be
we'll call on the deputy.
The occupation army
Has to stay up late
Working strenuously
to keep up the pace.

Armed camp
Occupation army
It's not enough to cite the poor sucker
We'll make sure he can't get out from under.
We'll tow his vehicle
And make him walk home.
With taxes and penalties
He'll be sure to stay broke.
If he recovers his vehicle
One thing is for certain;
Without fair and equitable law
We'll just do it again.

Armed camp
Occupation army
Revolution Army.

RIUA AKINSHEGUN

THE LOST/THE FOUND

I hunt for decayed wood
Objects to rescue
Trampled thoughts lost in fog
My lessons are taught
Through borrowed sounds in walls

I sit with People
No one sees anymore
I talk to children
Whose mouths have been painted out
I know their names

I found bicycle parts
An old love
A torn fingernail
Telephone wires
Ancestral memories

I have recycled flawed dreams
Ice cream sticks
A cracked windowpane
And the sun

I am not a parasite
I am the glue
That could hold you together
A scavenger

SITTING QUIETLY

When running from the world
I ran into myself
I was sitting quietly fighting back the tears

Even though
My heart dances with the beat and feet of a spirited child
Singing songs that can make the nightingales blush
Turning blues into reds
So why am I fighting to hold back the tears

I am the scent of a ripe passion fruit enticing you to open
My locks are twisting into gold
Weaving spells on the Gods and Goddesses
Yet, I am trying to fight back my tears

I mean
With the touch of a new born in my hands
I mold myself into my desires
I fly
But, but can you see I am fighting back these tears

I didn't know who that woman was
The one sitting over there so quietly holding back her tears
That was till you asked me about Rwanda
Till I realized that OJ probably did kill his wife
And found my people in denial
Till my son told me he shot his wife in the butt with a bb gun
Till my brother died of AIDS with the guilt passed on by Christians
Till I looked at my bankbook and found in place of money

Only fame
I tried to eat it
Till I remembered the young men dying on our streets or in
The jails
Till I had to report my neighbor for molesting his daughter
Till I received another rejection from the European art world because my art
is African rooted
Till Rosa Parks, the mother of the civil rights movement, was Attacked in her
home by someone she fought to free

Till I asked *you* and *you* and *you*
"Did you lose somebody in the Middle Passage?"

I didn't know who that woman was
The one sitting over there so quietly holding back her tears
I really didn't know
That was 'till you asked me about Rwanda

My body's taut
My face hurts

I fold my arms across my chest like an X as to protect me
My hand begins to soothe my heart
My heart is shaking
Quivering intimately
Tearing inside

Tears welling in my eyes
I can see no more
Blinking

I begin to rock and rock
First forward and backward then sideways
To the right   to the left   to the right   to the left
While calming my soul
While stroking my arms
My thoughts

Trembling
I try to talk
I can't
My mouth is too dry
There is a lump in my throat
I can fight no more

Tears gather at the edge of my eyes
Cascade down my checks into a storm
Hugging me

KIM BENJAMIN

JONESIN

There is a craving I have
Cause there's something missing
in marriage.
a jones come
like commitment
only he not a husband-
more dream
Than bad memory
passes my thoughts as frequently as
Two dollar bills my palm
comes willing to fix-
my squeak, too loud
he a drop of oil
applied on the rub
this get unusual- me and him-
like drinking brine
shameful as - licking ashtrays
we both do- and I don't tell
either
we unload ourselves
on the other's tongue
swallow like some do semen
like some do spit
tasting each other
on purpose
or not

HUNGRY

He is pulling into the driveway
Coming home from work
He will enter from the back door
Creeping like pesticide
Into the corners of our home
I will be holding my breath
He will not greet me with a kiss
Or touch me as he passes by
He will glance at my belly
Disgusted. No I am not pregnant
I am neutered. A house dog pawing the counter.
Timing fourteen steps from
The driveway to the door
Before he enters
I will have sopped myself
Up with bread hardened
from an early rise
Waiting since barney to be eaten
Used to erased traces of watermelon
Softened with juice, solidifying
A mid morning greed
I will know when he is near
From the nausea that will grow
And the fat I will feel
at 5"10 and 120 pounds.
I will make it though.
The knob will turn
And I will shush the water
in the kitchen sink
Wash the dirty dishes
And make sure the children
welcome daddy home

QUARTER MOON (FOR MY BROTHER, VICTOR)

He stood ten feet tall
even sitting down

He could lift me with one hand
so that I could straddle the quarter moon
and embrace its glow

His smile was the source of power
That lit Vermont at midnight
And caused my spirit to flow molten gold

His words I bottled like wine
in my mind and engraved them
with love from moon

He loved me first then showed me how
He is the reason I love now.

JENNIFER BOWENS

CONFESSION

(IN FRONT OF OUR MOTHERS)

1.
You are petrified wood in my mouth
Preserved you forever on my tongue
World Stage
October 13, 2002
My Mother
Your Mother
Sat side by side
Remembering a love like this

My Mommy Virginia Slims heat
Sing lullabies so out of tune
I thought Mahalia was doing 1ˢᵗ Baptist an injustice
Oh, just to hear "Hush, lil' baby, don't say a word"
Mockingbirds that never sat in my corner lulling me to sleep
replaced by the thump, thud, smack in the next room
Her eyes never met mine
looking at her hands and she swallows hard

Your Momma smiles a lot
But "who is this girl gon' take my baby away"
She feed you sweet bread and milk before you had teeth
Pinching her nipples
Slapping your lips into no more biting
You are now 14
Smacking your lips at no more food left
"I hope no one can hear the grumbling"
She closed her eyes and swallowed hard

2.
A sign reads
Removing rocks from the Petrified Forest is a crime punishable up to 6
months in prison and a $5000.00 fine.

My Father cannot read
He keeps that rock in his night stand to this day

I am my father's child
I stood that day and told the world of our childhood
Full of fear and beauty
the bitter cup
the hard bite
sugar water tears
and missing feathers on floors
Flat-footed in front of Mothers
Seraphim wings wiping tears and covering feet
Confessing the warmth of my lover's back and my sticky belly
We were no longer wet

Our Mothers cried
smiled
cursed
clinched teeth
and swallowed
real
real
hard

SATURDAY EVENING POST: LOVE IS...WHAT IT AIN'T...

Love Is...
Ain't fat booty naked white babies in the 3 Star Saturday Evening Post
No word bubbles telling of love and how he bought her flowers
and she saying so so beautiful
Well, sometimes it is

Love Be...
On you
Like Funk
Like hate
It is the bite in your chest when you answer your lover's cell phone and the
other party is saying all the wrong shit

Love Be...
The bloody lip on this page
A torn taint after birth and can't let baby go
and stitches healing very slow
It be walking for miles to see your baby on Massa' Jarmans plantation
Love that don't trust strange milk and choosing all death before you and baby
be a slave

Love Be...
Welling up in your mouth
Summers spent in the south
and the kiss you will never know again

Love is...
Ain't 15 on the phone and your daddy picking up the other end and curses
your both out

Love Be...
Sweetin'
Turning your lover's ear to something divine
Seeping into sheets like Grade A Syrup on Hot Ho'Cakes
Wide eyed lovers tender
To slice with a fork or eat wit' yo' fangers
Be snake charmer
calling out steam and body

Forgiving body
it be kiss
tips
lips
Full

Love Is...
Mary's greasy hair smelling of sweat and sweet oil
from cleaning her husband's feet
The noose
Crucifix spikes
A sore back from rolling stones from the tomb
The 4 elements in your mouth
It is resurrection
Fire descending
It is forgiveness
and I ain't done nothing wrong
But ain't that sho' nuff love
Halleluiah even for the Blind
It is the Light for those who see and those who will never
and all there is is light
and good good love

Love Is...
Ain't the falling
It is the energy for the journey

Saturday Evening Post
Print that if you bad...

SHONDA BUCHANAN

FUMBLE

and you ask yourself what are you doing here   again

and you turn away from the prayer stone with
two spiders spinning whispers on your shoulders
crossing each supple breast down to shoaled navel
creasing dank vestiges of pubic hair
and you walk to the edge of the sea with memories
as gangly and graceful as a child's first step
clinging to your spanish moss skin
as yesterthoughts do   and you know this is a thing done under the blanket
deeper than whalesongs forging bones out of sound
corral and silt
two fists wrestling with thunderbolts trying
to escape silver sheets turning bliss into jones
love into a nickel bag high
your language into willows that feed you

and you wonder which rock will fit all those words
you spewed about commitment, marriage,
wished you could have them back, swallow them whole
salt and all, when that lover or that one refused to
rain on your chrysanthemum as you took notes

and your nine year old princess peeks in the
candle-lit room, cuts the golden haze and
asks, mama, read it to me   and you wonder which story to unlace
for her shiny new-dress gaze
what to pour into those guileless palm
lines, still kitten whisker thin
never having known the spider
and sea and rock people
all vying for your attention
while you write   the last note to a mermaid
love song that only the oracles
can hear

HADYN'S SOLO (ANGUILLA I)

her body was an unbraided reed
in his hands
each spore envious of the breath
he whistled into the others
her slender arms
pleasure-weary from
his tongue and fingers
wading through her, trembled
and she opened her throat to him, vibrating
like a double-reeded oboe
undone, splayed on the henna shoal

licking his bottom lip
he blew into all her veins
plucked silver water bugs
from the moss that had woven itself
into her blades

each time he touched her
stealing her fiber with each salty bite
and pinch
she wanted to joke with him
about the dangers of too much
beauty, hoard her moisture, warn him
of the river reed within the ocean
he was unfurling

but underwater
his mouth already sticky with
her gauze
the quiet bubbles rising
wind wrapped around their eyes
she let him have
the last solo

DETROIT, CASS CORRIDORS, '92

(FOR ROCHELLE)

the homeless shelter where we stayed
that night in '92, with the other recovering
crack addicts, the whiskey-sweet war veterans

sallow-hearted hookers bent on changing
their lives, nursing scabbed knees
bruised women and their k-mart special kids
ankles/wrists/lips tattered/cracked, mid-west wind-blown

where we slept that night was a twilight.

beds packed in lobby downstairs
lined with hard arching bodies and hungry goodwill sheets
and all above them the placated stars.

vampire mist spilled over
oil stained curbs and cement edges of desperate buildings
split before our winter pace and cousin debbie's hyena laugh.

and i knew you was feening by all that
black coffee you'd gulped earlier
on an empty stomach, crossed with
cigarette after cigarette to get a high.

you and debbie each crumbled an empty pack a
kools Extra Menthol within an hour
of arriving at the mangled, piss-glorious
united auto workers hall, no longer a bastion
of american progress, just a building now where
recovering addicts partied at on salt-licked nights like these.

in hallway, the coifs of detroit women shined like
pistol-black bee hives, diamond-studs and razor blades tucked
there, glittering in the center of old pattie labell do'
flashing in harsh lobby light.

motor city grumbled
the monte carlo we borrowed hummed quiet with it all
against crack house stories

that time when debbie left her two-year old girlchild
outside in knee high snow while she used in jackel's
palace and when finished pointed
stroller towards home, or when your son, my nephew
held your head above the toilet seat
so you could throw up a high.
"don't know what I would have done without him."

but she clean now, you all clean.

you, janice and debbie, skinny as moonbeams
bright as swamp stars, poured out your laughter
like a kindergarten playground echo.

that night, against the cold blade of winter
the onion skin sky frozen above us
i saw you clearly
mist gone, stars hovering
a woman, young, in peril, her hindered elegance
strolling down cass cooridor in detroit
switchblade in pocket, but a little girl still
innocence parading away the shadows
who'd once touched her in the wrong places
and above
above
above her the placated stars

and we slept that night on a bed that creaked
and creaked under our starless weight.

outside too cold to breathe
inside, warm and safe. shelter.

we promised not to laugh at the worst of the stories.
We slept with the lights on.

IN THE TIME OF UNFORGETTING
(FOR RICHARD FULTON, DECEASED OWNER OF 5TH STREET DICKS IN LOS ANGELES)

in the time of unforgetting
one black flower reborn in the mountain of a snare drum's brow
when he turned in his brown paper bag and trench coat
one mecca-drenched turban wound around the fingers of a fat bass began to
play
when this salt and pepper dreamer/ not tryin impress nobody / rented a
piece of floor, some walls and slab of concrete

one hot cup of saxophone, two lumps of piano keys
and a dusky room filled with clouds came here

we were poets
with play sword words in our mouths
but he brought the music

we were rusty fountain water serenading
park pigeons, paper dragons, swollen-hearted hookers
beggin for mercy on they knees

he brought the black winter, seven holy years of sound
wing-tipped chairs, the vanilla bean field and a coffee moon

he heard us on nights when we thought no one was listening
heard the rifts in crack-addict veins, babies crushing their mothers
hearts as they pushed into this world

heard the memory of pool players last good knock
and scat and billy's seamless carnation
 falling out of her hair as she gave it all to us
when he came to leimert park
richard gave it all to us

grown men fell in love all over again against the
painted sunset

children running into the narrow, crowded room
 got tangled in the legs of bar stools

snatched whole notes out of the air and played jump rope with
mocha trumpet riffs

they danced in 5ᵗʰ Street Dicks' doorway with limber eyes
 knowing
one day music would come from their fingers
and they would say, what do you think about that?

he would tell them

i see it, the mango-shaped stars under chess players
pomegranate harmony filling a street
but don't forget where you came from
"i didn't"

so we didn't
"turn the music up" they say he said in his last light
and retreated to the edges of the universe as
the vibration pulled out the pain

he closed his eyes and saw his children
the black notes, the poets, sunken clouds
the winos, salty dominoes   the housewives and whores

all with melodies in their heads he'd helped create
 river sounds flowing from their
eyes that he'd woven into the dungeon of our lives

giants, drum sticks, and freestyle and ruby's
five dollar hug
he saw us   praying   with undone language
saw our mouths soothing dewinged angels
saw our hearts pounded down to two-cent dreams

it's gone be alright, he said
been there, done that

turn up the music

PAUL CALDERON

UNTITLED (FOR KAMAU)

In a dream
See a new man
   stand old in time unkept
       unkept as in what was forgotten.
  With sunrise over his left shoulder
     and over right
       a symphony of
          humming birds whisper his name
            beneath the wind
         a cacophony of Earth's crust
          (his color coded map)
        splits the ocean
         and from its middle
          rises his fist.
           w/ prophecy
             chiseled round his
              wrist. An omen
                come to life tense in time
              w/ sound clenched
                   between pale pressure
                      of his knuckles
              and the hummingbirds
               the hummingbirds
               (still)
               chimming his name
                "vvvvvv"
              A Sufi secret
              b/c
             vacuous space
               his
     The luminosity behind his eye
      (the third one in the middle)
       blinds ignorance w/ word.
        Change of season is child's play
         to this new man standing old in time

as he climb this stage
as Mohammad did the mountain
Each nail cringes
He climb this stage
with freedom locked in intent
and pain accepted as foreseen.
Now standing on stage
night in left lobe of his brain
day in the right.
Hummingbirds over his shoulder
your symphonic connection to truth
hushes in mutual respect.
(they are his peers)
The eastern lights pauses at the root
tongues its way from his equinox.
to hunck silver sounds
into his chin.
And w/ eyes closed
(third one in middle open still)
This new man standing old in time
cries a subtle answer in ear of a bow legged bastard
black boy
All of this world's symphony,
his army of healers,
the hummingbirds,
brings nine ruby scarabs from
his throne in Aknakam's tomb
They climb cold molasses thick silence
in his longues.
Each drone an intensity to harmonize
w/ the C flats and B sharps
wrinkled beneath his brow.
They are the music
beneath his breath as he
tearlessly cries
his memory
of a nigga knees
dancer

over hummingbirds
over
Earth crust cacophony

over
ruby scarabs
and
C flats and B sharps
and
cold molasses thick silence
He speaks to
a bow legged
bastard black boy
bopping his be
in a western time signature
amongst bowed heads.
vvvvvvvvvv
"earth is a prison, live your sentence."
"earth is a prison, live your sentence."
"earth is a prison, live your sentence."
earth is a prism
be light
live sound

vvvvvvvvvvvvvvvvvvvvv

be light
vvvvvvv   live sound

Now new man standing old in time,
knees all niggafied
bends to rock under weight
of two full saxophonic lips
snaps the nine ruby scarabs
into a celestial formation
that maps the path
past 125th and Washington
deep into the lap of a dog star
bouncing as would a ******
to birth
more sounds to
bunch up in space
to greet the moon
w/ hummingbirds (in a symphony still)
chiming his name beneath
a Suffi secret

And the bow legged bastard black boy
looks for an Orisha
follows through dream his shadow
his time
vvvvvvvv
his time
vvvvvvv
his
time
vvvvvvv

"flesh is a prison, live your sentence."
"flesh is a prison, live your sentence."
"flesh is a prison, live your sentence."

new man
standing old in time
turns
snatches
gyroscopic tilt
from earth's orbit
fucking up chinese star calendars
smacks
smacks bow legged bastard black boy
behind his ego
with mayan moon god

smacks bow legged bastard black boy
tells him
"Heal the garbage in your mind
clean your whistle
heal the garbage in your mind
clean
your
whistle
be light
live sound
be light
live sound
be light
live sound
make a space in your desert

for love."

new man standing old in time
    with night in right lobe
        day in left
   roughs a rocky step
        into essence of all
      Pulls out
        things men thirst for
        this mangle blood clot
          of gutter philosophies
        bow legged bastard black boy
          to see

new man standing old in time
        takes a single low gurgled bit
          from babbling slit lips of
            blood clot.
      shits it out
          onto concrete slab
  and with the rest
      he cold slaps
        bow legged bastard black bow
    knocking them both to knees
     and the
   new man standing old in time
      begins to pray

vvvvvvvvv

    "black is sound
        sound is black"
    black is sound
        sound is black"
   "color is a prison, live your sentence."
   "color is a prison, live your sentence."
   "color is a prison, live your sentence."
fuck the ologies
    be light
      live sound
        be light
          live sound

be
light
live
sound

and you
bow legged bastard black boy
heal the garbage in mind
purify what you will
burn all that shakes inside
BURN IT DOWN
be light
live sound
run slow with the clouds
taste the hate
in white eye
but forgive
don't forget
escape the paralysis
of analysis
be light
live sound
be light
THE GARBAGE
THE GARBAGE
CURE IT
IN THE MIND
RUN SLOW
BE LIGHT
WITH CLOUDS
LIVE SOUND
KNOW WHAT HUMMINGBIRDS SING
NOT MY NAME
PURIFY WHAT YOU WILL
BE LIGHT
LIVE SOUND
EARTH
FLESH
COLOR
THEY'RE ALL A PRISON
BURN IT DOWN
TO LIVE YOUR SENTENCE

BE LIGHT
BE LIGHT
BE LIGHT
LIVE SOUND
LIVE SOUND
live sound
cure the garbage in your mind

then the
new man standing old in time
like a chariot beneath the legs of a
machete swinging slave
whose tasted enough blood
dismounts the stage
vibrates his senses
into a thick mist to
claim a desert of love
on a crater of a moon

and the
bow legged bastard black boy

legs confident
un-bowed
un-bastared
blacker than ever
for the first time
stands
ready to learn
all that has gone
unsaid
beneath the dance of
the nigga knees dancer
and the sound of an
new man standing old in time
in time
in time
in time

time

time
ttttttttime
passes with on the light
he came
with phantasm's
hold
breathing from wind
of hummingbird symphony's
wings
vvvvvvvvvvvvvvvvvv
Light music sound

WANDA COLEMAN

OF CUCARACHAS & PEANUT-PEANUT BUTTER: A POEM FOR & ABOUT MISTER BIRDSONG

He is always crunchy, followed in crowded museums.
Yes, frottage et tois in dark movie theaters or nutted-up
at the racetrack when the jockeys roar as loudly
as the bettors—these are dramas in his edged-closer life,
someone approaching from the rear not to lift his
wallet but to tap him for a light and spare change.

Birdsong practices self-promotion by keeping others out,
unless they involve themselves by sitting under his
ass, or prostrating themselves before him at wine-and-
cheesers. When he inherits his father's fortune, he will
really show them who controls who speaks, replies, and
receives. His femm followers follow closely his every move
and dropping. He's even followed when licking his spoon
or eating out her liberal pan as she bows to the west.

Birdsong would run these hills, he would run this river,
two rivers, if necessary, to keep his position of power
over weaker bards. But what Birdsong runs best are
innuendoes, if mediocre ones at that, preening over his
victories, the voices he has silenced, the talent he has
alienated and destroyed, the prize he has seized for
himself, the trembling, tenuous egos he has trampled
with unmitigated delight, stepping up his surveillance,
until the better-gifted disappear. Until their excellence
ceases to offend him because it is unrecognized. Until
his maw is filled with poet bones, his pocket with tears.

Yet, as he will tell you, he is a man who respects God
because God made peanuts!

Birdsong is a man who wouldn't crush a cockroach,
who'd share his last peanut butter sandwich with
any homeless-but-cultured member of the subspecies.

FOR WOMEN WHO CRUISE THE NIGHT

—after Terry Wolverton

alone you speed where nothing exits
broken glass explodes into glitter
the asphalt is scarred with the spin of your wheels
escaping the wallpaper and bad plumbing
driving wide-laned empty boulevards
north to south, east to west
whispers of smoke climb the air from the bright ends
of your eyes—headlights or stars
maps dissolve at the edge of nostalgia
your hair and arms wind-kissed, bared & daring
the years screech & scream as you leave them behind
destination known as you traverse those inky ribbons of love
wary & slit-eyed
the prey that stalks its beast

KAMAU DAÁOOD

DJALI (FOR BOB KAUFMAN)

I
in the shadows of blue volcanoes
the broken fingers of ancestors strum
koras emitting frankincense

II
i sleep with a Senegalese blanket
of turquoise sound over me
it stops the helicopter blades from slicing up my peace
spirits sitting upon an orchard of notes
sprinkling my dreams
with promise
as i wait in this celestial cocoon for silver wings
remembering the lesson
dealt
in the sacred mud

III
each morning i read the newspaper
and weep into a pot of coffee
i muffle my whispered screaming
with the music of the masters
i find religion there
rocking in ecstasy
to the heartbeats of loved ones
i open my door and
begin swinging like young Muhammad Ali
i rest between rounds
on a bus stop bench facing east
i fight to knock out a nightmare
in broad daylight
the bus driver is a Sufi saint
who only lets you ride
if you got incorrect change
the Zen bell has rung

BLAKEY'S STICKS

I
I want to give Art Blakey's drumsticks
to some child without a father
to use as chopsticks
to pick the stars from beards of giraffes
sitting on milk crates
in front of liquor stores

men who have swallowed grief
and extracted the secret of seasons
men who have suffered and
found the stillness of a Mali morning
riding the red eyeball of
a hurricane
on a street corner in Watts

old ones who could stain young minds
with the lips of ancient songs
and make them friends of wisdom

these children of asphalt
blinded by grey and neon
tongue-tied with empty money clips
looking for faint footprints
of their home training

deaf to the voices of the old ones

II
I remember the flags of surrender
waving on clotheslines stretching
across America's abdomen
color dancing in a breeze of ghetto perfume
twisted ballet of Congolese sculpture
song in the Atlantic's darkest indigo
whispering pyramid of bones
at the bottom of the sea

come, ride the backs of purple dolphins
past the ghosts of the present
a spider waiting for you
in a world wide web
wants you to pick cotton in cyberspace
wants you to wear a bow tie
of yellow police tape
wants you to snort
the chalk lines on asphalt
thru a didgeridoo

children of asphalt
refuse to wear
the psychic beehive hat
swarm of conceptual killer bees
awaiting you at dawn
here where I is the first
and only letter in the alphabet

children of tarmac
seek out the old ones
with gold at the tips of their tongue
you will know them
by their scars

III
they will call you
when your mind is drifting
in the current of trends
your mouth spilling words
belching like an empty slot machine
their words will hit you
like a crowbar of light

they will pull back the concrete
show the naked breast of the earth
and you will cry
for the children on the milk cartons
and you will cry
for the butchered babies of Rwanda
and you will learn to ball your fist
and swing in the right direction

seldom are a young man's eyes
an old man's eyes
seldom are they skilled
as souls aged in struggle
you know this life
from looking at her face
light and the body of light
gloried in the fragrance of doers
builders, those that carry others
until they can carry themselves
the fire of truth
is an eternal flame
I want to give Art Blakey's drumsticks
to some child without a father

a moment of silence please

a choir is screaming eulogies
to a stadium of deaf people
is a grave plot
a hole in the earth
or a plan?

MICHAEL DATCHER

THE CRITIC, HIS WIFE & THE BRAVO CHANNEL

act I

the critic sits in orchestra pit
of her one woman opera.

knows her lines
but can't seem to recall his own.

she enters stage right
from behind god's back
wearing home training
crocheted by her father.

her mother paces the wings
calculating the velocity of forgiveness.

act II

no lavaliere, volunteer sparrows
leap from her throat, fan the audience
trilling her aria ear-to-ear.

her mezzosoprano womanist libretto
is not for sale.

act III

during the finale
diva keeps her wedding vows
in a hope chest
strapped to her retina. rehearses them every time
she blinks.

the star has fallen
for the critic. she hates when

he brings his notepad
home.

critiques her technique of
taking up space
like she is the man.

It's the critic who needs to be reviewed.

he concludes: she is
toni morrison as young aries.
king david in drag.
third string
on marley's first guitar.

the curtain falls.
when she leaves the stage
oxygen grows thorns.
the critic risks a deep breath.

JAWANZA DUMISANI

FORTY THREE DAYS

a girl play possum
in a church of corpses
shoulder to feet
under brutal siege
piled to a cross
teeth gnash, rigor
mortis agape

elder to mother's womb
sour with crimson milk
gorged to its waist
a wasteland's succulent fear
boots on the ground
drunk, turbulent bowels
on marble & magnolia

spring in Rwanda
shriveled beneath
diplomacy's broken foot
the gavel sounds
eight hundred
thousand
or three toast

genocide,
the saddest music
on earth
gnawed ears
a rabid hand
even gravediggers
are slaughtered

FATHER'S CALLING

Heaving marks our porch
Phillip Morris
Tangled in your fingers
A calculated leaf spat
Over summer's moist flame

Long as I recall
My left knee bruised
And you bedridden
But always facing your open door:
Look me in the eye when you call

Roped off
On your right side
Wired shut
From four sons
Mother punishing
Infidelity's arms

Hands in the kitchen
Dice onions
Without a blink
A flat toothpick
Parked between her teeth

All those tears at bay

A hymn synchronized
To an anvil on your lung
Across the table
You
Lower
Into her eyes

STATUE AT SACRED HEART SEMINARY

(DETROIT, 1967)

We yelped like torched dogs.
After the burning & looting
M-16's lowered
Tanks returned to 'Nam
I rushed before school,
as if someone
had rolled away the stone.
A black Messiah!
Face, hands; glazed coal
whitewashed & back again.
Thrice or more
even the alabaster foot
beyond his robe, clandestine
while the salvaged sleep.
Quiet men growing coarse hair
tarry through slits of patience,
black paint in the trunk
of a '62 Ford.
Saint & soldier play shell games
with a deity in the dark.

Momma says,
it's just a statue…he lives inside.
I glance at a white one
on our dining room wall.

For a moment
I'm saved.

RUTH FORMAN

I WEAR PRAYERS LIKE SHOES

pull em on quiet each morning
take me through the uncertain day

don't know
what might knock me off course

sit up in bed
pull on the right
then the left
before shower before teeth
they were my mama's gift
to walk me through this life

she wore strong ones
the kind steady your ankles
i know cause
when her man left/ her children
gone/ her eldest son without goodbye
they the only ones keep her
standing

i saw her
still standing

mama passed on
some things to me
ma smile sense of discipline
ma subtle behind

but best she passed on
girl you go to God
and get you some good shoes
cause this life ain't steady ground

now i don't wear hers

you take em with you you know
but i suspect they made by the same company
pull em on each morning
first the right   then the left

best piece a dress
i got

MAY PEACE COME

with each breath
each step upon the ground
each blink
may peace be called
each hand holding a hand
each blow across a face
may peace be called
each son running into his father's arms
each black baton across a brown back
each steel toe across a head
each forefinger pointing
a trigger
each falling body never to raise up
each mouth that will not close
each child calling a parent that will never come
each broken heart
each Bible clutched each Torah each Koran each holy book in every land
eye water spilled in pain
each blossoming belly despite us all
each you
each me reaching
to be better for our own self
each teenager learning her path head up back straight
each broken hand
each missing body part
each loved one looking
each safe safe bed
each sleep each wake
each new despair
each determination
each lapis night each amber morning
may peace be called
may peace be called for you my friend
may peace be called for you
may peace be called at one time
for all of us
and if by some moment
some slim chance
peace wakes
rubs her eyes to see who's calling

may she take one look
and fall in love
with us all

PERHAPS YOU'RE A SONG

waiting to be whistled
tween some man's lips
perhaps you're a prayer
folded tween his hands
perhaps you're a love poem
waiting to be written

or perhaps you're already written
n wait
for someone to decipher your language

or perhaps you're not waiting
not waiting for anyone at all

perhaps you're already all of these things
a song a whistle a prayer a poem
playing just for the beauty of itself

GOLDIE THE POET

A POEM FOR COWARDS

Everyday I see coward ass niggas
Posing as authentic gangbangers
Talkin' bout they got stripes
Their acclamation to fame is shooting a black man
But are any of these so called gangbangers
Willing to use their guns in the revolution?
Are any of these so called gangbangers
Willing to empty the clips of their 9 double m's
For the liberation of black people?
Cause to me
You ain't a true gangbanger unless
You gangin' up
And bangin' up
On the real gangsters
Operating incognito as representatives of a democratic society
Imitation gangbangers set tripping
On other imitation gangbangers
Not realizing that the real set trip is on those
Who have set you up for failure
Booby-trapped your quest for success
And tripped you to fall
Deep into a black hole of self-destruction
Nigga, will you set trip for millions of Afrikan ancestors
Who died in the Atlantic slave trade?
Will you and your posse, get into your Chevy
And down on American hypocrisy?
Are you willing to represent Black Power
so Brother Malcolm's death will not be in vain?
Nigga would you bogard for control of your own destiny?
Are you going to organize your homeboys
Into a clique of freedom fighting assassins
All across this continent?
'Cause if not,
Get the fuck out of my face.

PETER J. HARRIS

PRAISESONG FOR THE ANONYMOUS BROTHERS

See ya, I wouldn't wanna be ya?

See you plait daughter hair? See you massage son soul. See you spin their hours into gold. See you join the Y. See you coach boys & girls. See you ballet on the blacktop. See you maestro. See you Osagyfo. See you comrade. See you Rev. Doctor. See you teach public school. See you pick private school. See you open Freedom School.
See you. See you. See you.

See you baggy clothes. See you white collar down. See you wear holes in cold. See you & Homies chill. See you wax car. See you slap dominoes. See you mumble to yourself. See you answer back. See you tell the truth.
See you. See you. See you.

See you ride bus. See you drive cab. See you walk mall. See you clear counter. See you clean floor. See you hold baby's hand. See you hold woman's hand. See you hold man's hand. See your love in neon display. See you on the J.O.B.
See you. See you. See you.

See you done right. See you do right. See you live right. See you through my own damn eyes. See you fail. See you try. See you like we got the same address. See you bow tie. See you left coast dread. See you Black Caucus starch. See you push cart of cans. See you carry mail. See you guard doors. See you tame motors. See you barber holler next. See you farmer stroll rolls of food.
See you. See you. See you.

See you bedroom. See you boardroom. See you laundry room. See you talk shit. See you make me laugh. See you stress. See you call your baby. See you give her a rose. See you cook her favorite meal. See you call your baby. See you give him a rose. See you cook his favorite meal.
See you. See you. See you.

See you 100 Black men. See you Big Brother. See you Simba mentor. See you choose Allah. See you praise Jesus. See you drum Olorun. See you told what to do. See you run the show. See you punch that clock. See you speak. See you mute. See you cup your ear. See you hope. See you hustle. See you burn the flag. See your policeman's sprawl. See you up against the wall. See you slouch in court. See you Garvey. See you union. See you Duke Ellington. See you Maroon. See you brave.

See you. See you. See you.

See you stumble. See you graceful. See you dance. See you 9 to 5. See you after- hours. See you cradle bean pies. See you statesman. See you dropout. See you restless. See you portrait. See you *collage*. See you emblem. See you word like song. See you stutter Rodney King. See you opinion like it's fact. See you old man. See you black boy. See you link times two.

See you. See you. See you.

See you jailed. See you caged. See you tamed. See you pain. See you fronting. See you lamping. See you want. See you need. See you dissed. See you Blood. See you Crip. See you Brother. See you sober. See you loved. See you peace. See you home. See you listen. See you love. See you *on it*. See you faithful. See you chumped. See you challenged. See you change.

See you. See you. See you.

See you confide. See you fried. See you still got my back. See you sick. See you used. See you beat. See you offed. See you suicide. See you blues. See you ballad. See you jazz. See you straight. See you gay. See you with sister. See you with blond. See you America. See you Europe. See you Africa. See you redbone. See you Wesley Snipes. See you serene. See you home.

See you. See you. See you.

See you city. See you country. See you tired. See you silk. See you denim. See you dare. See you risk. See you hip. See you get props. See you surge. See you Turn. See you Tuned. See you Man. See you living. See you *Live*.

See you. See you. See you.

I definitely wanna be you.

FULL GROWN

hair on a woman's fingers & forearms
blues crocheted into sun-up cradle song
I suck my thumb
stretch my baby hands
wishes hum in my palms

a woman's unshaven legs
my nipples become aching candles
I close my eyes
sway to drone welling
from center of my chosen appetites

hint of a mustache   thick eyebrows
my breaths fuse
full underarms   treasure below exposed navel
my sex arcs

my hallucinations whimper
face down in sweat-scented roots
beard lost within untamed blending
sliding cheek along curving ankle
licking wayward strands framing naked toes
hand tangled up in breathtaking veil

hair on a woman's body
blurs my oldest incoherence
stirs incandescent my my my
I faint standing up

SHADOW BELOW

hides her right hand
in the shadow below her belly button
teases the shekere' between her open legs
her hips jolted by individual music
playful smile hips me to independent surrender
slide my invitation into her salsa
dip my hips with swagger subsonic
as a Chitlin Circuit rhythm section
sloping bodies curve into each other
like pussy willows blown from inflamed saxophones
I beg her to teach me Spanish with her tongue in my ear
stroke Chinese sign language along my tingling lips
I lick Arabic from right to left across her steaming chest
stutter in shuddering Japanese in time
with the gliding of our indented bodies
we exhale Yoruba into the satisfaction of glistening arms

laugh out loud
after another exhilarating vocabulary lesson
sing a babbling version of Shorty Long's Function at the Junction
jab our middle fingers toward the ceiling
to shoot down the helicopter shredding our skin deep revue
kiss until our sanity drowns out the sky
her right hand hovers near my nose
I am hypnotized
slip my left hand into the shadow below her belly button
lose track of common sense education
& my social security number
return with her to the craving place
where the only documents
have already been signed   sent downtown
& lost in the system

nobody can punch us up on their computer screens
nobody ever hears from us again
we are never even missed

LeVan D. Hawkins

DESTINY

(A CONVERSATION WITH LANGSTON HUGHES)

Excuse me for disturbing your peace
But I rob dead men's graves
Seeking bones of wisdom
Angry fists on the periphery
Have left me wanting.
The women who do men's work
Cannot teach me what it is to be a man.
I migrated north seeking the manna
Father withheld from my dinner table.
Northern men versed in Leviticus
Slammed their doors upon my arrival.
I have wept ink upon a forest
But the brethren would not hear.
I scraped my words off the page
And returned them to my heart.
Still, they would not listen.
So, I have come to you, Poet
To learn what is to be a man.

The Poet replies:
    I cannot teach you what is God-ordained
    But I will tell you
    The brethren will become lost
    And a scout will come searching;
    The words will be there.
    Thousands will stay behind
    But someone
    Will come searching.
    I welcome you, friend.
    I, too have wept ink upon a forest.
    A table has been set for your arrival –
    Smile and accept your fate.
    There are workers in the watchtower –
    They will guild you.

Unleash your words and
Turn them into a simple song.
Take your heart and let it play.

REGINA HIGGINS

SUBURBAN BLUES

Suburbia sprawls wide legged
Against backdrop of utopian skies
Varicose veins of rush hour throbs
Crisscrossing between valleys and
Ridges of sleeping foothills to
West Covina, a city in the mix

Tequila sunsets sooths tired souls
Hands caress Coronas, a swig away
From this hot Mamacita with
Low-riding dreams of slow drags
Browned skinned brothas in du-rags
Booty-bumpin, heart-pumpin
Grooves with sweet moves
She's dying for a trip to L.A.

This sistah's dreamin of jazz
Sizzling on back grilles
B. B. King, Muddy Water blues
And greasy spoons
She's dreaming of Crenshaw cruising
With dropped tops and no stops
She be leaning old school with no rules
Hip Hop, R & B, just enough boogie
To unleash rhythms of the night
But for now suburbia sprawls
And West Covina sleeps

YURI HINSON

SILENTSPARROW

hush little baby, don't say a word. . .

for you there were no lullabies
no kiss goodnights
no sparrow songs rising with morning light
but i mourn you still

the delicate memory of imagined hands
fingers long against the promise of veiled tomorrows
you were the god child of an earthly union
misfit fruit of taboo desire
and your graceless conception was blurred
by the antiseptic memory of euthanized shame
but in truth what death is painless
what loss not felt in guilt and regret
for deed and debt to life itself

i have been scraped clean of the proof of you
bled out the residue of you
laid waste nights and tears for the grief of you
while sorrow stood to claim your place
at my breast full of fallen laments
nursing this despair growing healthy in your stead
and i am beginning to wither away
scattered to the four corners
on wings of your songless sparrow
still searching skies and memory
for your cry

yet with all the noise of trivial existence
your silence will be my life sentence
a fitting penance for the crime
though i am neither judge nor jury
it is the flock of spirited songs
whose harmony seems flat without your voice

that will wrench my heart
at the unveiling of every tomorrow
your hands were sent to reveal

stay with me silent sparrow
and your wing will heal this hollow
forgive me martyred child
i have no words to claim defense

JAMAL HOLMES

HELP

I don't mind being married
I just don't like to have someone
responsible for all my sexual good times
I think that that's way too many bags
for just two people to handle
I need a bunch of folks
it's like trying to do the Wiz
with just Dorothy and Toto
I'm into grand productions

ADAMANT

So I was explaining to this lady
how I was married
and how I can only do it with her
if a group of my friends are involved
we need dominoes, and alcohol, and a game on the big screen
I even insists she bring some friends
because my marriage is sacred

WENDY JAMES / TCHECONSASE

KENJI

Outside
He is an arbor
above me
fills me with roots
waters me
brings me roses
drinks me like bourbon
tells me
why the night is black

This year brings me
All his notes
And lab books
I am voracious
We talk long
genetics, synthesis
meiosis

Inside
we look up
across velum pages
He is seventeen
A cell in a book
on a library table
caught in the lemon circle
of lamplight
Peeled back
to the show
beneath the membranes
Everything dividing
out of itself
in quantum phases
a picture
on a quiet page
like music

with its black
stemmed currants
waiting to spill
from someone's throat

I am a serious shot-glass
secret
the red-eyed swallow
A smooth assault
on the chest
Followed by the cough
and deep inhalation

I am twelve
and he is becoming
a man
who holds my name
in his mouth
like ginger candy
brings me the sky at night
on the roof
and the lazy August
crescent of the
waning moon
like orange rind
curling its arms
around Venus

PEARS

You,
were once my enemy
I rode you down
And slew you
Along the Yellow River
You,
were once my love
And cradled my head
On your thigh
Before severing it
From my body

How then
Will I love you now
As though we are unscathed
Let us open the book on each other
And vine between the pages

When I see you
on the promenade at noon
buying pears from the vendor
I know you
By the back of your neck
The turn of your wrist
When the coins fall
And say to myself
Here, again is my enemy
Let me open my shirt

FARJ

not in my bed
But on the ground beneath
A wide moon
that has cast her net of ice
across the desert

you moan like a burning man
At 4 a.m.
Stunning me
To stillness
I turn leg over yours
remembering

The broad leaved mullein bows
a snake's eyes
Peel back
In the pitchy midnight
Where the path of your breath
Deepens in the bottle-blue
cavern of your chest
air opens and closes its fist
like a newborn
Above the crying bone
where bullets sleep
warm as sisters
within your spine
torahs of lead
Telling Black man stories to my fingers

I envy them
Their secrets
The raw wealth of your blood
white silk of your bone

quiet as clay
in the pall of sleep
A scratch at the tent
farj
and You can't find the door

that leads away from me
out to purifying water
and the mat
With its powder of ice

JASON LUCKETT

JACKSON, MISSISSIPPI

he sipped a glass of water
brushed a dark fist across his forehead
they used to live next door, he said
I don't see them much anymore

inside his son was working on the family business papers
he called it Frank Turner's Garden Bouquets
his son's son drove by in his yellow school bus
and made all the kids wave

it's not simple
where hate existed, patterns remain
the black neighborhood in Jackson
the white neighborhood in Brandon
no one's crying and few are tryin'
they'll sooner forget the struggle
than begin to understand

Felix lived out in Brandon
he looked kind of isolated out there in his house covered with gates and locks
but he said, I can make it here in the white part of town

the public enemy, for every falsehood you raise questions
people talking loud in Jackson
people talking loud in Brandon

no one's crying and few are tryin'
they'll sooner forget the struggle
than begin to understand

you can talk to yourself--what is the good?
you're isolated
no walls to cross, no need to cross, we're ok here
ok

so I finally sat down on the porch next to my grampa
and asked him why
30 years after the death of Martin Luther King,
blacks and whites didn't talk to each other much?
he said,
dialogue's not the question
we've got a home here, it's not that we fear
it is simple
no need to move, so why should we?

it's a circle in Jackson
it's a circle in Brandon

the black neighborhood in Jackson
the white neighborhood in Brandon

no one's crying and few are tryin'
they'll sooner forget the struggle

at home warm inside with no reason to revise
they'll sooner forget the struggle
than begin to understand

JOSSLYN LUCKETT

FIFTH STREET FIX

philippe vieux was 22-going-on johnny hodges heavy
i'm minding my business
ordering my sweet potato cobbler straight, no vanilla chaser
when phil's devastating "solitude" stream down to the kitchen 'n
make me switch up and beg for a la mode
I'm thinking some old dude up there layin' this tenor hurt on me
makin' my lactose intolerant behind insist on this digestive lunacy
makin' me ache for that impulse bossa nova coleman hawkins joint
my ex made me memorize then hijacked when he moved back east
along with all my jackie mclean...
but that's not this blues
confused, cause dude on the flyer outside look barely legal,
i turn and look for richard
who's leaning back on his stool
noddin' off to phil's deep time serenade
he cradles, rocks the pork pie hat
collectin' the five bones to get in
we all know it won't weigh much by night's end
but richard rests peacefully
knowing he's given a home to that
future heavyweight haitian upstairs
fightin' his way to lion status
solo after solo

philippe vieux was 23 when eddie palmieri
kidnapped him from leimert
ain't had sweet potato cobbler since
richard gone
horace gone
billy and his samba smile
left the park too
what's a sweet tooth jazz fiend like me
supposed to do?
so low
sooolow

K. CURTIS LYLE

WORD FROM JOHANNESBURG

I receive the believer
Who was charred by the fire
I accuse and accept
The perennial liar
I take pleasure in setting
The day on top of the night
My historical measure
Becomes the wedding
Of the black and the white

The people decide
Not political whim
Human beings once blind
Look out over the rim
They see the weeping
Of blackness
They hear the confusion
Of Boers
They feel their knees once
Rubbed down to bone
Now redeemed at the shores
of counsel and home
That care could workup
Into the marrow and blood
That love could become
The herald
Where hatred once stood
Is a tribute to patience
And to faith and to man
Recognition
That courage is at the heart
Of the plan
It could all end tomorrow
or become the fact of the ground
You make the call
Tell me brother and sister

If what was lost
Is now found

Reconcile and then wed
No more guilt
No more sin
The jailed and their jailers
Close the wound
Heal the limb
Hatred is futile
Revenge is absurd
This is the word
From Johannesburg

CURTIS SPIRITUAL SUNWOLF: OR THE CONVERSATION OF DEATH

After I stripped your flanks
with the streak teeth of my street razors
I renamed you there
ritual suicide
and you fled into autumn like
ritual timber assuming a posture of snow
Through the insular winters I drove you
and your brothers and sisters
toward the Eskimo highlands
toward the eskimo hatred of solar joy and destruction
I was the ritual Sunwolf
and you were the ritual Doe
bestowing the conversation of Death

Drinking the blood now dripping from your bowels
like the awkward hot bellows of cold howling spirit
collectives
reminds me now
that it was your choice to be driven
that it was your voice that called me down
from the mountain of hunger
to fight
that it was your holy gesture
beginning the decaying dialogue
that must always lead
to the conversation of Death
I am the ritual Sunwolf
and you are the ritual Doe
staring straight into the conversation of Death
I threw you down into the white desert
of stomach cramp defeat
I cut the tendons of your lower leg
to destroy your mobility
I watched you die all night long
because you asked me to show you
the spirit that kills
the real spirit
the one that asks for your ultimate will

and then dares you to refuse
to walk the ultimate way
Now the spiritual Sunwolf
meets the spiritual Doe
in the deep conversation of Death

I am asking you for the stoical spirit
                    for the black solitude spirit
                    for the haunted earth spirit
                    for the depth spirit flying to heaven alone
I am asking you to consent to the gradual breakdown
of body and tissue and marrow and blood and bittersweet soul
I am asking you for your life
in the sun now
in the dark tick-click of primal throat gesture
in the laser wolf fang expression of pain
sinking deep into the bone of your nose.
I am asking you to give it all up
in a matter of seconds
to the spiritual Sunwolf
                    cloud coming over
the spiritual Doe
I am demanding that you give up your life
to a secular primitive pocket of light
to me
the wolf missile
the mangled cadent spiritual Sunwolf
the delirious hoop fang dancer feeding on blizzards
to the sucker of successive meat-muscle rottings
to the angular father of fire swaying through night
in clay pools of dread seed and wolf sweat silence
I am imploring you to do the right thing
but I am obstructing you too
because I want to be more and more
of a spiritual Sunwolf
                    cloud coming over you
as more and more
of a spiritual Doe
bestowing the final and real
conversation of Death

A.C. LYONS SR.

VOICES

barriers break
the smack echoes wildly
he struck her like lightening

and she fell hard

the flash lingers
shock ricochets with lightening
throughout her scull

and he wants to strike her again

a life's frustration
has charged his hate
and the b i t c h
had the nerve to challenge
what's left of his manhood

the way mama use to
and every other heifer
he got stuck with
just because he did it again
that thing
that one little thing

it use to be so overlookable

but her mom was a fool
took that crap from pop
and she ain't having it
not her
not a fool
the thought burns
taste bitter
made her noxious

pissed more than hurt
she hexed him
with the oil
of opened palm unforgiveness

and his cheek is toxic
one more bruise
inside

another woman wanting
him to explain
what he doesn't understand

he wanted to cry
but daddy said
tears are for punks and sissies

so he became lightening
and for a seconded
it felt good to be powerful

but something started to hurt
again
fear begets angry

he had to squint his inner eye
from the pain
from the shame he had to ignore

so he made her a scarlet river
her mouth
the flood gate opened

one more reason
for her to despise the species
to
see i told you
to forge granite
higher
thicker then last time
but not so wide

a box must be tight
to not feel the canker spread

and oh my God
the children
they forgot about the children
frantic
screaming
this stranger
this new daddy
doing what daddy use to
just before he disappeared

God
make this one disappear too
prayers

scares and bruises
materialize like magic
metastasize
faces contort
necks become rubber
a womb screams

children's hearts are defeated
by each thud of a knuckled hammer fall

the police are on their way
ms smith shrieks from up stairs

but it's too late
the house
in bloody disarray
them in the kitchen
her mother's voice
reverberates
angers
with each tearing scratch she hopes on
a niggah ain't worth a damn

his arm collapses her neck

his father hunts
be a man boy
let no bitch push you around

a fork in his thigh
makes him stop
thin stainless steel
in her reach
beckoning

not a thought
no worries
her hand becomes stainless steel
between his third and forth rib

no pain
just shock

every one in shock

and it is over
and it is over
it is over
it is over

and the children
what about the children

oh my God

3-21-95

california grit under my skin
louisiana cedar moss
dripping from my brow
feet heavy
with mississippi red clay
me
swaying
in the breath
of her south texas hurricane
cupped hands
catching
arkansas pine
she brushed free from her hair
while perched far sighted dreaming
through west coast sunsets

I asked
if a seder red clay palm
melted in a hurricane pine sunset dreamer
would we create deities

she cut me three times
just below the neck
licked clean my wound
then bore me twice
to answer

I grab her tight enough
to steal breath
lopped off running shoes
hers and mine
then chanted libations
deep into her safekeeping

now there's babies everywhere
tracking red clay
seder sunsets on their breath
pine and grit in their hair
and hurricanes
hurricanes in their eyes

YmaSumac Marañón

LOVE IN THREE SCENES

I
In her father's kitchen
A bitterness hung between them not yet done
Sitting at kitchen's table where
No talks had ever taken place
No graces had praised family
No food had ever been passed around
Not to her
Not from him
A stranger to his kitchen
His plates
Tools that served memories

The spice cabinet with salsa de locoto
Antichaja
Aji rojo
Names that fell from studious lips
They did not roll off her fingertips into her food
Her llajua a blend of blood
Never quite enough of her father

She only knew of the hunger
The craving that moved his youth to a new land
She was a stranger to her father's daughter
Her youth blind to the whispers
left behind his ears by time

Her father
Unyielding
Sunburned coffee
Dense like an old wooden armoire
Handmade by artisans whose fathers taught them their craft
in the cradle of their mother's arms
Every curve, handle, hue bronzed
safely kept the secrets of their name

while standing in strangers' halls and forbidden bedrooms

Everything holds a symbol

Goosebumps stood at attention when her name left his lips
A tension between these goosebumps and his invitation
to eat of his food
learn at his table
toma mi espiritu
Sitting at the edge of her chair
like a shadowy jaguar of the forest
ready to leave in retreat when noticed
back to distant shores
where picture postcard hammocks swayed over soft moonlit sand
 holding cracking eight year old figure as it howls to the moon
looking for Papi in each white ray
wanting him home where she waited
 arms never closed
always expectant
He never came home and now, was too late

II
Years later in her father's kitchen
Backpack sagged on worn chair that heads the table
Green from revolutionary thoughts
she didn't need to ask where tomatillos were
she found them quickly in the drawer cupping the sink
Tonight familia would be over to tell of news of roots long ago cut off
re-planted and grown over again

She would make the llajua
that would spice the tongues to speak and dance all night long
Her father already busy moving around her and the stove
peeling potatoes, cutting chicken, grinding garlic
bringing flavor with bare hands
There was music in their movement he taught her long ago
hot-humid days
when summer revolved into a night dance floor
and familia watched her move into her role as daughter
They bumped and laughed when their stories collided onto the same stage of
rallies and midnight meetings and boycotts
He was the cloth of her life worn as a head wrap

in the heat of a blaring sun
  He protected her from lost faith which time carefully wrapped in coca leaves
These he gave her one at a time as one finds pearls in oysters

She was building her own armoire
carefully crafted from the blends of her life
hues of russet, garnet, gold
markings before undiscovered
now lay bare for future artisans to learn
  This was their home
  one they created from dirt, tears, spit and sweat

III
An unexpected year later
  Midnight silver rays
cast a muted light on her tear-tainted face
following the pool that trembled under lip
swirling into a thin thread
landing soundlessly on the kitchen table

  There was nowhere to go
familia had long gone home
shadows compete
for the golden light of the chrysanthemums
littered at her feet

  this was all she knew to do
    no llajuas to make
  no spices to blend
  no stories to tell
    fires were out
  and tongues cannot speak without a flame

  Where had she missed the signs?
  Her life had been of symbols
    born to translate in between the lines
    to find the veiled and bring it to light
  She was his greatest symbol
  How did she miss this last one?

Where were the signs?
  Where did they show on his tanned, strongly set face?

Which line was the bearer of this desertion?
How would she move through this kitchen again?
What dish was there left to be made?

When armoires retire from use
only an absence
 a shadow
is left in the space behind

KEITH ANTAR MASON

A WALK TO THE PACIFIC

perhaps i have known sin best of all, my raw right foot on the earth, i am
against, the mouth of this breath and all of my eyes are looking at other
naked black men, fifty years from now, my borders, my skin, my teeth, my
bones, will not assume that i could have mattered to any one but my own
children, i look at the faces of other black men, hoping to find, my sorrow's
real name, i look for me on postcards, and in memories of summer bar-b-
ques, and heat/ when i feel like this, i wonder
what trouble has come to visit the hands of other black men, told me that i
was ugly, too big, too huge, my left leg hurts when i walk, the streets, i see
how they look at me, i feel homeless, this wind is cool
and spring has started like the space in a pimp's walk. i have no alibi,
no relations with anything god that could save me, from this, i learn
that winter will not surrender, at all...i purchase the sunday news paper, to
look for all the books just published, how will i read them all, the ones that
strike the hammer of my own thoughts, the voices that will get heard, how
they will know themselves, chapter by chapter, my face, in this crowd gets
looked at, i am suspected of something, i am hulking, my clothes fitting too
tight, i do not seem comfortable, here
i keep walking past the restaurants and the noise, there is this statue
of santa monica, i call her yemanja, i touch her base, the ocean is still beyond
me going there, to meet her, i gave back the driftwood,
that i bathed with for years, shaved my head, i am nothing to look at really, i
wanted to be beautiful, but i am big with history, i carry it around with me,
if my tongue was god's would i have these fears, there is a slave castle on the
shore of afrika, somebody i loved, got lost in the dark and we have never held
hands, I am trying to hold hands with them, all the time, and there is this
part of me, in jail afraid of dying of aids, even while i write this note, i look
at the newspaper and wonder again, how will i read them all, and who will
remember, this body, i have stretched it beyond use, i am looking in the eyes
of brothers passing, if they notice me, i know that i am alive still,
haunting myself for recognition like a tooth ache, i have never had reason
to love myself, i realize this when the wind rushes pass me as well, it doesn't
make me smile, i will walk back home, still not able to grab the hand of
someone who will smell how i loved her. perhaps this is
sin.

GEOGRAPHY OF A KISS 1

some men learn how to kiss behind bars with a plate of glass between them
the past the future ticking two fingers a child's smile behind a long ache
they say it like a promise i love you it does not hide the bloody bruise of
cell extraction the five member team has trained for situations like this for
this is routine a black man's fist lit   in glaring harsh illumination   there
is a certainty of guilt no error has been made from the first time of lift your
balls the guard wears gloves spread your ass cheeks   he checks for weapons
jerking knees in the air they hose you down sometimes ask you to choose
which book stays with you   it's all good if only you could eat words is how
you judge which one you keep i wonder who gets to keep your letters the
pencils you wrote them with they cover you in a white sheet you are going to
die alone in there in your body no matter how many witnesses come   your
mouth is full your lips look sweet as if your mother kissed you right before
this moment your words jack hammer at the glass keeping us apart this is a
murder you say and i understand this old fashion notion of death keeping us
apart you understand with brown eyes guarded by thick arching eyebrows a
trickle of blood wiped away from your scalp your black veins thick and raised
above the muscle of your flesh   jacob lawrence would use deep browns to
paint you i see no hope in your eyes yet i think this is my surrender thinking
of ways to save you i am not in texas I'm in your heart and i want to know
your blood who was the last to kiss you your tongue rolls to hold you
while you trembled still full of life no priest around for confession the sin
is clear i wonder about your feet like a fetish is this your destiny and what
does it mean   could you not sleep the night before will you throw up your
last meal i can not cry for you somehow you were too handsome to cry for
grainy pulp paper pictures fade out the force of your last words   you were
never a desperado because you lived in texas   you refused to die a slave so
they beat you again one last time a broken arm a rib cracked something was
wrong with you the eye witness saw that something was wrong with you
and we all know what it is   your skin brown   sweaty   black fine hairs
growing out of pores your elbows just a little darker your second toe longer
than your big toe we all know what it is you suddenly stop breathing one eye
opened they bury you in texas a man who knows   the geography of a kiss

LYNN MANNING

IN THE ABSENCE OF LIGHT

What the fingers know
the tongue knows best:
Of lips and cheeks and nose and brow,
It bears little resemblance to where the eyes live,
Light and shadow
Color and contrast
Fall away in the absence of light,
Give way to tactile terms:
Firm, round, full,
Silken, moist, muscular.
What the tongue knows
It conceals from the teeth
Salty, tangy, waxen, warm.
What the teeth discover
of nipples and neck,
Inner thighs and baby toes,
Backs of knees and ear lobes,
They savor as for the first time,
For this is the first time,
Seeing you this way,
The first time Seeing you at all,
Curved and convex,
Quick and hard,
Slow and trembling,
Pleading and demanding,
Vulgar and ethereal,
Drowning my senses,
Consuming my soul.
In the absence of light
I lose myself
in you.

ELECTRIC MIDNIGHT EMERGENCY CALL

Time tramps
Wide-eyed and slack jawed
Toward electric midnight;
Having peeped the fraud of 'New Age' mysticism,
I have come full circle
And dance among purple pyramids
To the chamber music of suburban bathroom chemist;
I am para-sailing the synapses—
On an elector/chemical cruise through tall cotton;
I am
OUT THERE.

The phone rings;
Its cord,
A pulsing axon to the 'real world;'
Its receiver,
A volatile neural transmitter,
A plastic explosive awaiting my touch.
I gingerly lift it from its cradle.
The ear piece shatters
Flooding my apartment with the sounds and scents
Of my mother's drunken poverty;
Her desperation looms huge and horrible
Just beyond the grasp of my rational mind;
I have to reel in the ectoplasmic filaments
Extending from my fingers;
Command Miles Davis and Herbie Hancock
To cease stirring their foul smelling Bitches Brew,
And allow this six foot thick shag carpet
Time to retract to its original height.

I say,
> "O.K. Moms. I turned the music down.
> What was that you said?
> You shot the mothahfuckah? What mothahfuckah?"

The room expands and contracts—
In rhythm with the controlled heaving of my chest;
The apartment walls become my exoskeleton,
Provide me the volume to contain

The images pouring from this shattered earpiece:
Some where in South Central L.A.,
Just a loogies phlegmatic flight from skid row,
My mother stands,
A smoking gun in one hand
And my throbbing ear in the other;
Her old man lies tossed and twisted on the filthy floor,
Dying of bullet wounds
And being far too loud about it;
He's oozing
Ancient, alcohol saturated, indigenous American blood
All over their worm rotted floorboards.

I think,
        Can't the septuagenarian mothahfuckah stop bitchin'
        Long enough to die quietly?
        I didn't make all that noise when I got shot;
        when I lay oozing
precious African American Irish Mexican hemoglobin
        into the beer stained carpet of that Vine Street bar,
        my sight sucked down the black hole of a .32 automatic.

Mom shouts,
        "Damn it, bastard! Shut the fuck up!
        Ahm tryin' to get yo' ass some help."
I ask,
        "Did you call an ambulance? Did you call the police?"
Mom says,
        "Yeah, but I can't get through.
        All the lines are busy. That's why I called you.
        may be you can get through up there in Hollywood.
        Get them to send somebody down here
        before this old bastard dies on me."

The colors in my apartment
Shift to red hot awareness
Of L.A.'s socio-economic inequities:
Those who most need help can't get it when they want it.
The South Central Saturday night shootout
Is well under way
And plenty of blood will be oozing
From newly torn button holes

Before dawn shines its search light on the carnage.
I light a cigarette
And inhale the entire contents of my room;
Frustration pours from my pores
As rationality takes residence.

I say,
          "Just stay cool, Moms.
           I'll call the paramedics as soon as I hang up.
          Leave the gun in the open and get away from it.
          Call me back if you don't hear from somebody soon.
          If they do show up,
          Call me from the jailhouse when you get a chance."

The Hollywood emergency operator asks questions
That test my tenuous cool:
          "Who are you and what's your involvement?
             Why didn't she call on her own?
             Why didn't she call from down there?"
Through rapidly growing teeth and hair
I hip him to the ramifications
Of tax based emergency service,
Check book police protection,
Bid him long life in Primrose Lane,
And hang up.

The rescue now in motion,
I return to slow motion.
I remove a schlitz stalagmite from my cavernous fridge;
Start that Bitches Brew to boiling again;
Climb back up into the bell of Miles' horn,
And am myself
Blown away.

JOSE MENDIVIL

BITTER DIRT

It covers the earth
around the one rose bush
she keeps from wilting.
That bush planted
in memory of her husband.
He never returned from Belgium
from the Bulge snow battle.
His body buried
at an American cemetery
and dirt from Manzanar
sprinkled on the thorns.
They pierce her winter hands
as the Santa Anas kick up the sand.
And she sees him
like the last time she kissed him.
The dusty internment desert
shading his waving arms.
Once a national risk, now 442nd GI.
Her tears caught microbes
and her hands clenched
the soil he stepped off of
as he boarded the bus to bootcamp.
She would keep it, give it to the rose bush.
Bitter and Love,
ingredients protecting
the roots and stems all these years.

BLOOD LINE

Love slipping on black jeans.
Love buttoning up that brown beige, flannel long sleeve.
Love pulling up a pair of well worn, tan, round toe cowboy boots.
Dry farm, raising only corn and squash rain will give.
We are ranchers who stock Winchesters in our saddles, rope and brand,
corral and butcher.
Hunting deer, barefoot in early March or in those black leather moccasins
Tio used to slide on like it was medicine to make him invisible while tracking.
Bless every cartridge, pray deer people consent to our bullets in their necks.
Bless their hides they make warm.
Bless their skulls they make dance Holy Week when New Pascua Yaqui
elders lead gourd rattles to center of the universe, just south of Valencia Road
towards Ajo Highway junction.
Bless their blood we drink, fills our bellies, soaks into veins and nerves our
brains remember this animal that runs with us, ran with us on paths we
depressed into Earth for 30,000 years.

We have uncles in our family trees belly crashed in North Korea, mined
bombs in Vietnam.
Our mothers in Canada barricaded bridges, overturned RCMP Crown Vics.
We have heroes raised flags on Mount Suribachi.
Place flags on our fathers' graves honor elders who said "We are Indians."
We are nations, running into each other at urban Powwows, Disneyland, in
downtown L.A. nightclubs, on a gravel paved road near entrance to Lower
Brule in mid February.
We are horses bumping the corral chewing hay.
We drive the next construction site singing to Freddie Fender on K-FROG.
Drive cross country runs on I-40, sleep in our Kenworths at 2 A.M. on off
ramp shoulders.
We chew asphalt, our intestines absorbing stories of unpaved great basins,
filtering life labyrinth of everyone before, their laughs and tears percolating
up into redskin hands turning the rig onto next rest stop after a long day's
haul.

What looks like a ditch from the ground is clear when seen from the
air, a road that coupled desert cities long since departed into tongues of
grandparents telling stories to children sitting in circles in front of televisions,
so that our babies will know why they are.
We tattoo our arms, painting our bodies with BIA tribal police uniforms.
Feather our crew cuts at museum shows.

Feather rear view mirrors on family road trips.

Feather that T-shirt we sell to half Apache, half Mexican park ranger browsing at the annual UCLA Inter Tribal.

Cut down that tree without permits we make homes we need them.

We are gangs of workers pouring cement and concrete, welding and sweeping, mixing iron and rock.

Remixing all that was already made, our powdered snake meat medicine pouches hanging on our necks, underneath brown beige, flannel work shirts, as we drink coffee at the ten minute break.

Drink coffee like we swallow blood of freshly killed venison, blood dripping on hooves stomping old footpaths.

We masticate animal's marrow, digesting its stories till they turn fluid, pumping through our hearts, filling our lungs with old oxygen, ensuring another 30,000 years.

SEQUOIA OLIVER MERCIER

RICHARD

I explode
at the gate
where grief stands
stumble on the pain
the possibility
of losing you

yellow gourd on my head
filled with seed and vine
and new belly beginnings
is a rattle
and a womb I shake
to call the sun

I am haunted by sorrow songs
vomited at your feet
unraveled and suicidal
when we met
your smiles
surveyed scraped knees
offered band aids with blue stars
to catch my blood
while I sifted gratitude out of
graveled disappointment

chewing a rainforest
of Jamaican coffee beans
in search of Stanley Turrentine's
sugar
sitting
on your corner of the world
my intention grew straight
enough
for me to stand
and call myself a poet

I scrape my bones
for answers
for cures
for words
to pry away the hand
reaching for your life

hot sand roses
prick the healer
whose work is not complete
I kneel in my own blood

on this Thursday afternoon

I lower the gourd from my head
fill it with
lemongrass
lemon balm
names and numbers of survivors
sage and a mantra to stop time

I give you my eyes
floating fingertips
massage words
from your throat

I give you my hands
to loosen knots
of interrupted sleep

I hold back tears
because you are still smiling

I listen deep
breathe words
as they form
in your eyes
round with
silk and simplicity
beautiful still
with no teeth

you tell me
Leimert Park
is the place
you most want to be
time…eyes…hands
elusive cures
hot sand
blinds
the seated soldiers
guarding your door
I want to run cross the table
piss on their chess
scream peace
into salty beards
then I remember
this is what men do
when they cannot cry
they study war

but who am i to judge
how others love

an invisible hand
folds tears
under my tongue
lays laughter
in trench of sadness
crisscross my forehead
like old growth forest
holding more secrets than it tells

I thread fingers thru
unabridged collection of history
water drum in my veins
riffing a funky fever blues
in search of root
un-severed
in search of
supplication
invocation
a prayer
to stand above

this
Autumn chill

SONGBIRD IN THE VILLAGE

I fall up
into your eyes
when I least expect it
loose and unrehearsed
curl myself
in cumulus cloud
of your hair
pray for rain
Pleasant wisdom
on this June nite

tangle feet in tussle
with my higher self
tongue bell
swings in my ear
songbirds gather
a winged ventriloquist
throws my most private thoughts
into the air

the music
circles our heads
falls
softly
upon us
we are all
feathered
and shining

tonite
my love come down
like ready watermelon
fresh from Georgia field
burst open on my head
black seed make music
seduce shakeray
shimmying in my chest

I hold reservation
gripped between my toes

and parallel reality
somewhere
pressed against
the floor and
Lucy Florence sky
a purple sun rises
with a peace sign in his mouth

I know this mouth
one long Summer
when time was counted
by the moon
I filled it with breath
And pieces of new sky

the world beyond
is here
I am drunk
from it all

tonite
the songbird
gave us wings
made it hard
to remember
we
are not
lovers

RHONDA LYNN MITCHELL

BORREGO - A LOVE POEM FOR THE DESERT

I wish I had forty years to wander you
With an ounce of water to my name
And a storm resting on the tip of your tongue

My footsteps would pester your streams
Polish its blue laughter into the blush
of this springtime afternoon
And after all that laughter
I tip your oasis and take a sip

And your subtle beauty is my daily portion of manna
Blooming yes in the springtime
Tiny petals of yellow and white
Spoons and dusters for fairies

With forty years to wander you
I would mold the scent
of your desert lavender
Into a calf
And worship it
Until a petty god threw stones

PRAYIN' FOR RAIN

It was the wisdom in your eyes that beckoned me
did a dance and called my name

Rhythm in one foot magic in the other
I floated in on jasmine scented angels wings and stood

before you
watched words spill from anxious lips
pushed by throats with anxious tongues
that would slowly strum the distance between us

And you tried to buy my time
used play money promises non negotiable notes
not intended for use in the real world
and all I could spin
was the circle sound of your name

and I chanted it
and I chanted it
and I chanted it

'til Pentecost days
turned into holy ghost filled nights
and I was filled with the spirit of you

and we became god and goddess
and we became priest and temple
and we became man and woman

and I was satisfied
my fascination worn thin

worried knees knelt on the altar
the distance between us
and I lifted my eyes and prayed for rain

MERILENE M. MURPHY

SOMETHING TOLD ME NOT TO OPEN THE DOOR

&
sure as i didn't want to remember you
in my kitchen with a bleeding knife
coming down on my face & ten other places
there you were
day after thanksgiving
which nobody with first nations blood
or empathy calls thanksgiving
except if they're slaving like a fool
for a plantation day off

it was the next day i knew
walking down from emergency
down the street back to my life
all 11 stabs stitched & everything working

it was then i knew why
when something told me not to open the door
i let you in

you are my brother's son & an orphan
your mother died when you were eight
my mother brought you to our best intentions
here is the water of love she said
grow
here is a roof & food we said & light
you said you read the high priced books
you did well in the high priced school

the day we had the peace l.a. gang truce
poetry block party in leimert park
when you were 10
you wrote peace poems
a year before the day i let you in

when you were 18
you wrote this:

A field of yellow when the sky
          turns gray

An urge to look up at the sky
          as we wake up each day

Sometimes I listen to the birds
          as they chirp

Sometimes I wonder what
          life is worth

i let you in because i knew you knew

IT BOTHERS ME

i.
not counting zero
the times or ways a child might
die in a land called rich love
not counting
the ways a no count so-called president
fixed his mouth to say
worthy wars
with his addicted to money self-loathing self
mixing gas with blood
even if money junky bloodstains *do* ruin those
outrageously tailored trousers & totally shatter
the myth of always clean bulletproof limousines
cameras only ever catch him smiling
plunging deeper down
not counting
a long lineup of a money junky's tired heroes
all with the same first name stu & last name pid
their lives the wilted matches tossed at
ignorance's feeble torch
theirs the tired tears turning blood to
wreaths & neatly folded speeches
bless the poor dearly dead
they sanction
pity the high cost of wealth cannot ever be
buried without more loss
unconvinced
i, too, am tired
i barely make an after-work last stop at
the corner store gas station on
the way in
they tell me over the counter
this is l.a.
the kid got shot
right there
right in the head
mr. chung complains
helicopters, 20 cop cars, four hours no sales
louie's worked at chung mobil forever or
at least long enough to see

worthy wars raise gas pump prices again
& again & again
louie co-signs *yup*
right there next door in front
right in the head
mr. chung's fingers blast his temple
right in the head

ii.
foretelling, telling, retelling: reality
foreshadow dream peels skin off the day
the sleeping boy's absence sits on
the counter between us
a boiled potato we cannot eat
fear we'd belch & his mother'd come sniffing
off a long busride home from west l.a.
tired from scrubbing toilets &
folding other children into her love
none of us wants to be the one to say
i had two dreams
a day ago
a bullet whizzed through
a sunny yellow day & his brain
two weeks ago:
a poorly lacquered canary chifferobe with
bulging bellied drawers
one ajar
its golden handles jangling & the about to be dead
boy rummaging for a mother's soothing voice
looking for the right journey socks
the ones closest in touch to the rose petals of
his sister slipping him one of her last two anything
please don't let her cry now
i swallow the dream i had two weeks ago
it was broad daylight
the chifferobe had faded away
executioners circled an about to be dead boy
sun poured down hot useless sympathy
a futile attempt to melt away what was coming
someone on the killing team stood behind
the victim & sung his favorite song in
his right ear just as

the masked executioner danced before
the about to be dead child
crossed his heart
held his kissed fingers to the sky
& shot
cigarettes & beer in tow
i leave mr. chung & louie
pieces of dreams falling back to
the ground rose petals
across washington boulevard
a block west of rosedale cemetery
a circle of guadalupe candles outblazes
the coming purple of evening sun
trickling golden tears down a
neighbor's gate &
the tallest palm where
a boy's body fell & fell again into
permanent yellow

iii.
it bothers me you died so young
it bothers me you died right here
across the street from two dreams flashing
i saw it coming weeks before the downing shots
weeks before you sleep out a bullet's lullaby i weep
it bothers me i learn your name now you're gone
i wish I'd touched the alphabet spelled you in life
i wish i could have helped you right our dreams
little king born to this i wish you blue skies flowering
majesties of quetzal flying over bling bling
i wish you humilities of ma africa's smile singing kisses
the bliss of every child winging native american wisdoms
when an elder laments the death of children
more than regret salts the wind
i wish sun shines on us all ways
here is the yellow of my hope:
our broken hearts will mend
i stand here with my silly wishes
rainwater tears dropping the seeds of this poem
roses soft & strong for some place better
& you little king still breathing

ART NIXON

JU-JU MAN
(FOR JOHN COLTRANE)

How can you stand there &
How can you sit there &
Be negative in your blackness????
When so manymany of your kind
Your same black-kind died for your sins
Mens who handled God's love & saved you a piece
Blew you a God-kiss thru tarnished saxophones:
OUT OF THIS WORLD Trane stood
Describing mean scenes in his Ju-Ju madness
Possessed by God
Possessed by God
Trane at the apex of priest MU/scians
Make'n wicked nigger-noise in the west
Watch'n wicked critic white mens drop dead in'61
'cause he plays the Lord's Prayer backwards....
Make'n it happen anywhere: hot ivory offering
In the niteclub of the universe,
Niggerlips sealed into the mouthpiece.
Hot ivory. Piano smoke: BURN TRANE BURN!!!
BURN, BURN---Legba & Damballah & Ptah come
Full circle out the bell of the baddest horn---
BURN TRANE, YEAH conjure up the spirits...
& Malcolm, who I thought wuz dead, stood bringing light &
Nat Turner sung a deafening love song---I saw Harriet---
Felt her breathing in the stereo: TRANE TRANE TRANE
Coal TRANE hauling strange niggers into my living room
Done conjured up the spirits
Done conjured up the spirits
Unfamiliar faces of full-blooded Africans/long gone/
Dancing in the music
Dancing in the music
Voices and visions escaping from the stereo/
Nailing down the black-blue pain of AFRO BLUE nights.

Slack-jawed awe of flying Negro saxophone fingers
Charred black by molten keys/ his horn a glowing ingot
Of supersonic tenor screams/ chasing chord progressions/
All the way back to ancient African Kristallnachts:
Delicate hair-raised, chill-boned blues-scream
Piercing of nites/ village terror/ civilized white
Nite sticks & clubs waylay unsuspecting Africans
From the nite bush/ pythons writhing/ hyena scream/
The sound of sub-Saharan skulls cracked/ black feet scatter/
Africans juke-move/ stick 'n' & move/ stick 'n' move/
Africans stutter-stepping the pitch black/end run around kidnappers
In dough-face wit they own white death masks they can't take off/
Unfulfilled legacies broke down B-flat in low moans/
F-sharp pain of shackles/ buckled down
African wrists
African ankles
African necks & knees....
Big boats slow rocking sagging deep in sea-green foam
Portuguese wood groaning the weight of black gold, choice black booty
Of: gutbucket/ zoot suit/ razor slash/ sky hook/ call & response/
Peanut butter and plasma/ bebop & fertile jelly-roll/ Jessie Owens & James
Brown
Ali, Smokey&Baraka/strange-looking fruit/ seven principles of *Nguzo Saba*
smuggled in the mouth, tattooed on the tongue of Maulana/ the talented
10th/ 8th 16th & 32nd notes as sheets of sound gitdown gitdown gitdown
TRANE:
Blowing compassion & mercy, love & forgiveness on the horn's upper
register:
KYRIE KYRIE KYRIE ELEISON
KYRIE KYRIE KYRIE ELEI---TRANE:
Blowing PURSUANCE as El Haj Malik Shabazz! Azan! Allah-u-Akbar!
TRANE blowing jewels from the heart of the lotus blossom:
AHM MANI PADME AUM
AHM MANI PADME AUM
AHM MANI PADME---TRANE:
Blowing homage to the power beyond the beyond, and beyond the GREAT
beyond,
Page 3. of Three
And beyond THAT beyond:
GATE GATE PARA GATE, PARA SUM GATE, BODHI ISATTVA!
GATE GATE PARA GATE, PARA SUM GATE, BODHI---TRANE:
Blowing SUPREME enlightenment revealed in The Daishonin's dharma!

NAM MYOHO RENGE KYO
NAM MYOHO RENGE KYO
NAM MYOHO RENGE KYO
NAM MYOHO RENGE---TRANE:
Blowing past gadget & me/chan/i/cal & dig/i/tal im/a/ges/ of / the
world, past the blues/ funk, hip-hop & even jazz/ blowing & screaming past
perversions of self-hate & alienation,
Past whatever white people call themselves AND me &
TRANE plays and
Plays, and
We know we are saved.

BREAK DANCING FOR THE POPE--
FOR MARY ON VALENTINE'S 2004
(...love is a secret whispered between two fools....--Anonymous)

I love you. And it's still scary,
Making my way in the world
By the flickering light
Of the fires in the heart.
And the longer we have loved each other
The more that the reason for our love
Seems no longer accessible to either of us.
To love you
Is sometimes to have had
The satisfaction of a secret skill,
Like spiting into trash cans from a distance
For filthy three-pointers,
Compulsions to wash the hands, turn the back,
Deny desire, stretch out the arms towards
The next sunrise with regret & hope & tears....&
Underneath it all/that comforting noise/muted drone
Gathering in the gut/vibrating up the throat----
Forming as a new religion, an unmistakable articulated prayer,
A life-saving litany of "thank God I'm alone again"
----up and on out through the lips
Like the recycled, stagnant water---tired and tepid---
Piped out of beautiful garden statues.

II
Yes, it's scary because
We really are the show,
And each other's audience of one
Captured in the Plexiglas of the
Visitor's Room for "losers in love"
(mirrors have not exactly been our best friends,
swollen witnesses to the 15 years of our collected girth,
yet neither of us has yet to breakout in song
nor seriously shut down all the auditorium lights....)
Finally, for us/we have no choice but to dance
Where we are the music and the lyrics:
Where night & day cancel each other
And the world dissolves into

A rioting, dazzling, blinding
Mardi Gras of infinity,
Where atoms are as big as suns
And time has the mind of an idiot savant
With not the slightest intention to obey: Today,
This is where I love you,
And must confess
Where I have always loved you/having long ago
Crossed over the line/stepped out of bounds
In front of the huge Bay Windows
Looking out on God's Property: a trespasser/
Where any direction is the right direction
Any thought of you is the correct thought
A million choices is the only choice.
This must be the only place where it is worth being loved,
And the only place where being love counts,
Because this is where we love best/
The only place I can adore you/who will
Probably always show up strapped
With your gene for psycho Gemini scandal,
Lying through your teeth,
Whispering the truth with your eyes,
Giving me your last breath before I ask.

III
...I am here
I rest my head on your belly where you are, and feel the
Soft growl of your stomach where you are. Yet in your dream
You know it is me: chasing your hunger. Cornering it. Feeding it,
With warm, fresh baked, buttered kisses from the basket
Of my large warm hands...

IV
In our world
We are never apart:
By now/we know that the reason for
Our love did not follow us into this lifetime,
But we know how it looks,
How it works
And how it feels:
Thru 180 days of lockdown glass
& soundproof darkness,

Questioning your/my sanity on
Unforgiving benches on visitors' day,
Disoriented, necktie flapping over the shoulder
Like a hysterical compass needle/ moving into
& thru the warp in the black hole
Out the other side of the universe
That hurtles crush-sped, full-lunged life-need
Faster than the speed of thought, Light & Dreamtime,
Through the invisible vector that empties
Into the common insanity called L.A.,
This viscous place of sluggish vibration,
Where the permutations of grit, dirt & darkness
Pass for thought & spirit & love,
Where we must first & forever
Honor & polish our thin but golden linkage,
Cupping our hands over the tiniest flame against the wind,
Hopelessly, sometimes arrogantly,
Crazy in love, crazy out of love,
A tag team of two,
Willingly, lovingly,
Having met the Buddha &
Killed him in his color-coded jumpsuit,
And not the least bit self-conscious....
Waltzing for beggars,
Break Dancing for the Pope.

V. KALI NURIGAN

I'M RAISING CHILDREN

i'm raising CHILDREN
i'm not the farmer's daughter
raising CHICKENS
to be slaughtered
not the sharecropper's child
raising CANE to be
CUT DOWN
i'm raising CHILDREN here
RAISING
not California singing dried fruit
raisinettes
not raising STRANGE FRUIT
to hang from some oppressor's tree
i'm raising PRECIOUS fruits
to grow HIGH on the vine
PRECIOUS FRUITS reaching toward
the sunshine
raising the fruits of my womb
to multiply   by five
to stay alive
i'm raising CHILDREN here.
no little bo peep
leading her sheep to be slaughtered
these are my daughters
these are my sons
i'm raising CHILDREN y'all
raising them UP
ABOVE the flood waters
I AM the crossing guard
cross me and YOU"LL be sorry
'cause I'm raising CHILDREN HERE
between rock and hard space
betwixt slim and none
'tween fatback 'n' no slack
i'm raising CHILDREN y'all

the instructions are included
DON'T FOLD SPINDLE OR MUTILATE

the instructions are included
DON'T FOLD SPINDLE MUTILATE
NEGLECT MISUSE OR ABUSE

just follow the instructions
like you do OGUN and the MOON

just follow the instructions

cause i'm raising CHILDREN here

i'm raising CHILDREN y'all

i'm raising CHILDREN here.

NANCY PADRON

SPANGLISH & SPIKANESE

I am collard greens
Chinese laundries &
steamy summer subways
uptown salsa
swept sidewalks
& morning smells
of Spanish Harlem *panaderias*

Fried fish and grits
hand-churned butter &
backwater blues
woodstoves, oil lamps &
storytellers named
Arabelle, Adele & Big Mama Sara

Black beans, fried bananas
& yellow rice
rosary beads, candles &
the black statue at the door
called *La Caridad del Cobre*
Adorned in gold
by aunts in white
Narcisa, Erundina & Tata-Mami

I am holy-roller sanctified Santeria worship
at Bed-Sty family reunions
biscuits & gravy at 4am
the fried chicken left on the stove all night-
fresh city plucked chickens-
wrung necks and feathers
fight the wash for space
on sagging alley clotheslines

I am the funeral parlor and the projects
- a two-casket existence -

the sweat lodge ceremony and the
ancestor rock, jumping the broom
the First Nation cousins:
Dancing Feather, BlackWater &
Rain Comes Late
Red Bird Spirit children
cursing Columbus &
Christianity

I am the cigar rolling, conga-playing
Havanisto
in Ybor City factories
I roll my sweat in Don Quixote,
Marcus Garvey & Karl Marx

I am the one-breasted
Amazon Archer:
the rite of passage
the rain forest surgeon
the jive-talking Jamaican cousin
draped in gold arrogance
& history

I am the Hail Mary &
the Yemonja
speaking in tongues
the drum-playing
guitar shouting
spirit-calling cadence of
Sankofa
Sankofa
Sankofa

Dance
Kneel
Pray
think of Samba, Merengue
& the Hully-Gully &
Lord Have Mercy *carambas*
I am Spanglish & Spikanese

E. J. PRIESTLEY

5TH *STREET DICK'S* (#14 STORY)
(CIRCA 1994)

we were kicking it
slow motion up on the *Front*
told Dick, 'Round people don't die square.'
& change is the only thing that really last
old Dick shuffled the cards
told me to cut & I did
Dick said, this here is Bid Whizz—Rise & Fly
Gurantee & the Joker'r Boss cards
Six-Low take out Six Up Town
No Trump take 'em both down
All cards to the board
Trumps board themselves
No talkin' 'cross the board
6 cards in the Kitty'
Luther walked up
Cup of Espresso
Cause now it's Dick's joint
Told 'em put on some Charlie Parker
He did: Bird & Dizz
Dick say, Luther, what's wrong with Sylvia?
Niggers eye-twitch caught up in the sliver
Key Man shrugged
Told Dick, 'hell if I know
Key say, 'she finished U.C.L.A. at eighteen
Hooked up with some O-Fay
Went to Big Apple
Got to trippin
with no ticket one night
Drums say:
Gray Boy fed her too much Acid'
Dick say, 'Look in that Kitty,
I swear fore god I'll kill you
I laughed n' set it down
We'z sittin up there smoking & jokin

Dick puttin his cars together
Say, 'sh come coppin homeless
I went, 'Four Low
Partner say, 'get the fuck outta here
Somebody say, 'who Slyvia?
Dick say, 'Five
'the Poet?
Luther's cousin
Not Plath, fool
I say, 'typical German though
Dick say, 'how so?
'sober, austere, desperate—wild goose steppin
nigger-eye caught up in the berry
Dick say, 'she claim she kin to Luther
My partner say, Five-Low
I say, 'Five-No Trump
Dick up n eyes me
Put his cards down & passed
Dick say, 'I told her straight out,
Syill, you handle no pan up in here
Not in my joint
I picked up the Kitty
Say, 'what about it, Luther?
Key man say, 'what about what?'
I say, 'she kin to you?
Key man say, 'I don't know
We all bust out laughing
Dick say, what, Key,
Tell me you don't know your own kin?
Key say, 'Fuck you, Dick'
& that crazy Sylvia
& the horse she rode up in here on
Dick say, horse? You mean nag
Folded my Dead Book from the Kitty
Asked Dick what he meant by that?
Dick say, somehow she called a cab
I say, 'called a cab?
Everybody eyebrows up
Eyeing one another
I say, 'how she homeless callin cabs?
Dick say,'search me
I say bag lady—my ass

She on the grift to my thinkin
Workin some angle]
Partner say, 'who the hell homeless
Can afford a cab?
Dick say, homeless, uh-huh she claim
Key man say, get real
& we dug some Charlie Parker
went Seven Out The Front Door
Rise & Fly
Playin Bid Whizz
Kickin' it up on the Front
At 5th Street Dick's
Got back in time to hear Gwendolyn Brooks
Looked around & Dick's still trippin   on Sylvia
Told him 'fore we split,
'Round People don't die Square, Dick
& change is the only thing that really last
now that's straight out

In Memory of the Late Richard Fulton, the owner & operator of 5th Street
Dick's Coffee shop in Leimert Park (taken from *The Lazarus Gospel, a novel—
non-fiction*)

5ᵀᴴ STREET DICK'S REVISITED

(CIRCA 1994)

a basket man
40 ounce
the empty breaks
in a gutter
no time he takes
to sweep the shatter
& pushes south on Crenshaw
jusst off Century carjack
the one who shot
the woman's two-year-old
the night before
& in the head
no hailstones
but a bullet mindless
as new slug leaves the chamber
trigger men
the news is
they ain't returning
pulling it off
just launches the now
beyond the zero
the street is psychic
& little pieces of us all
died with him
on noisy steps
without porches
in dead end alley backups
down on any street no exist
that spoke in tongues
taught the ancient language of the stone
bag ladies
& fragments of people
remnants of who they used to be
or never were
but glass & falling
wedded to a dream
that wakes up in a sewer

JERRY QUICKLEY

CALCIUM RINGS

The hills of Altadena
held the bones
of my cousin for more than a year
before hikers found him
The animals had gotten to him
the police said
it must have been a drug deal gone bad
the animals had gotten to him

They shipped his remains home to the family
in a box
the size of a small suitcase
too small to possibly
hold his memory
or the landslides he left behind
or the pints of whiskey
his father began to swallow
to keep from breaking

Lost in an urban outback
looking for anything to mute the sirens of regret
Like aborigines sniffing gasoline
stumbling towards detox farms that harvest angels

Lost histories of
dreamtime and middle passages
drowned out by broken bottles
vacant lots and billy clubs

I will find myself

Lost among the vowels
creating modern mutes
looking for new metaphors
with old lies

Lost among travelers who can't hear the call
of the didgeridoo
From their new homes inside of glass stems
malt liquor bottles and squeegee empires

Lost sounds of the prairies
a night so clear and black
the stars touch the horizon on all sides
you try to hear the earth spin
you feel the heavens curve
with faint promises of mercy
I am so devoid of human touch
that a knee in my back
is a blessing

I want to hurl his name into the hills
and wait for him to walk out -
whole again

I will find myself
Wandering the streets in daylight
holding a lantern looking for one honest man

Lost among rookie cops whose idea of safe sex
is slipping a condom over their nightsticks
before using them
and throwing my cousin's bones on the floor
as though their random position
will tell the future of our tribe

Lost in the sheets silent transfers
blood tests and first world triple cocktails

Lost among the provisions
lists of survivors
hair conditioner and film rights

Chasing ourselves into the thickets
becoming reeds to hide from ourselves
as dogs chase their tails

I will find myself

My runway is the kaleidoscope of Chavez Blvd
My prairie the grassy expanse of traffic islands
and my cool blazed profile lying in the grass
high mesa is found on the nighttime roof of the parking structure
where I set up my telescope and I spy
3 puerto ricans from the hood
wiping their names on the moon's surface in Petroglyphs
with cans of Krylon

And my prism tells me
there is something better
waiting for me

I will find myself
In the bones of my family
and the whispers of the hills
in the bones of my family
and the whispers of these hills

SMOKE AND MIRRORS

Forests burnished by sun and wind
struggle along its edges
its core defined as much by what is absent
as by what it holds
bonhomie vivants and acid cleansers
Aztlan is not arbitrary
but the people making its choices are

Los Angeles
strip it and fill it strip it and fill it
The digging
The constant digging
the thresh of oil derricks
miles and miles of those big
dinosaur heads
slowly bobbing
drinking all those fossils
all that blood and iron and oil
pressed up against the orange groves and the sun

a group of indians stand in relief against the sky
a wounded picket fence across a ridgeline
they take one last look
before cursing the lot with a handful of smoke
and disappear further into the desert
again
and again
and again

the stark beauty of joshua trees plowed under
they didn't have the feature movie value
of palm tree silhouettes
swaying mops
casting their long stick thin shadows
across the bungalows
slap dash and disappearing
so fast
it's as if they were

being destroyed
by the movement
of the sundial trees

And always the rush of new arrivals
ceaseless migrants
pushed through the mortar and pestle
of real estate barons
and the vacant eyes of boosters
they're not here to build their own dreams
they're here to be cast
in the role of invisible servants
their stories hinted at in their calluses
and way the lines of their hands
hold dirt and light
with their hope tucked neatly into
the rings of their irises
while their pupils shout loud mysteries
one more day for my son
one more day for my mother
one more day for
one more day
one more day

and still they come
how can a place without a past
possess so many snapshots of the future
mountains sprung from cramps and spasms
tectonic plates move mindless as sharks
while saving us all from the magma
it's only river a concrete channel

and still they come
it's gunshine and cowboy cops
with overly sophisticated uniforms
it's mountain lions and live psychics
it's tamales and a beach
it's freedom on a leash
it's barcaloungers floating out to sea
it's derelict mass transit and
thirsty enough the drink the whole Colorado river

and still they come
it's a culture slide under a microscope
24 hours no commercials
except when you have to breathe
it's a science lab with cable television
it's a vending machine and
mostly you don't have any change
Los Angeles
Pico Aliso
Pico Union
Sunset Blvd.
Alta Vista
Sierra Vista
La Cienega
Vista Del Mar
it's a Rubik's cube
in the hands of a blind man

and still they come
zoot suits, lingerie, bellbottoms and afros
It's the Jazz stuffed into the sidewalks of Central Ave
it's fruit trees in backyards lit up
by helicopter search lights
med flys and malathion
it's bonsai trees and cactuses that eat houses
it's a culture rodeo complete with the clowns the bulls
it's the flat basins of tarmac and sun
it's a crip with a gun
face screwed up to your car window
shoutin' what set you from

it is a mug shot on the cover of Vogue
it respects nothing and it respects everything
it values In This Moment

a beautiful and awkward child
too wise for its years
too much the smart ass and teacher's pet
it knows it all
it knows how beautiful it is
how to whisper and when to shout
how to strike the perfect pose

touch this papi you know you want to
you want to try and hug film-stock and smoke

why are you trying to figure it out
what's in it for you
sit back motherfucker
don't play yourself
this is Los Angeles
and if you're still asking questions
then you don't know shit
this is Lost Angels and
the riddle is the ride ese
the riddle is the ride

ARIEL ROBELLO

HORIZONTAL GEOGRAPHY LESSON

your bed is the edge of the world
where we lie
unnumbered
unhinged
tracing the outline of your United States map

you are determined to know their capitols and order
rainbow quilt of stoic rhombi
how free the coastal states
their furthest seams defined only by volcano and sea

my index finger trails the Rio Grande
its mud bleeding down my chest
your thumb leaves coyote tracks
guides for those that follow

this land is ours

as the politicians sleep through our anarchy
we buy back California for my grandfather
Louisiana for yours
here manifest destiny dare not brand its legend
arrows pointing toward an imagined west
a muted south, a lonely east, a frozen north

all trains are caught still
no freeways flap close enough to wake us
this night reparations are collected in pores
opened by mutual love for a fifty-first state
free state shape of waning moon or twin bed
state with room enough for two

ODE FOR THE MIC

through time you stand a shepherd's staff
herding profits and derelicts
heroes too, souls intent to do right by the world
an obelisk under red light
spit in your pores
you stand to make love
like vigilant stela in Copán
resurrecting history from deep inside the jungle

I've seen men catch seizures after just one dance
hurling through their concrete façade
I've seen you make them cry
still they come back
with whooping cough confessionals
in whispers, enraged
the pay off is hearing their name called

you are Pied Piper's flute,
anchor, Maori spear,
bayonet, lightening rod,
faultline trembling,
Liberty's spine aching,
thermometer rising,
bass string pulled tight
playing the scales of our breathing
our over-heating
our melancholy brand of New World jazz
an antenna calling all channels home

and when the city burns again
you'll prove scepter to the Black Star of Africa
digging center to where sanctuary waits

and when the bombs drop too close
you'll turn pole vault
lifting us over and out of despair

and when they finally discover the dissidents
planning revolt in your lair
you'll turn Katana blade

'til death you'll stand
and should that day come
we, the poets, will have our own Iwo Jima
raise you from the soft skin of death
to your rightful post, center stage, all eyes

S. PEARL SHARP

WHEN BILLY DIED

they heard him
when he put down
his sticks

they came

when Billy died

they came
to play him
through the night
3 trombones
2 trumpets
14 saxophones
4 flutes
7 piano players
3 poem singers
6 bassists
9 drummers
and didn't need no
e-mail

they came

May 3, 2001
Los Angeles

ALL MY QUEEN MOTHERS

(FOR BERNICE, BEAH, FRANCES, GWENDOLYN AND...)

All my queen mothers are stepping
out to lunch,
breaking bread with God/ess
sucking on adam's ribs and
smackin' down sweet potato promises
we did not keep.

All my queen mothers are stepping out
traveling to a camp meeting
where they will do what women do:
talk about their children
chanting our
chanting our
chanting our names
making meal of our meant-to.

All my queen mothers are stepping out
gone dancing
the blood springs
the breath is endless
the step is light
free now
swirling around the fire
free now
stomping down expectations
kicking up a laughing day
joy in their toes
a tantric dance
free of temples with
technical difficulties
And I, well
sometimes I feel
like a queenmotherless chile...

Queen mothers gone to
film school
making messages to reach us
during the commercial break

Queen mothers gone
shopping for answers
left some issues on the stove
note says heat and complete

Did you expect us to be ready?
How are we to fill this canyon of insight?
   with plants/ or photographs/ and memory?

When the space you left has
sucked our eyes dry
then we will see you keenly
wiping blood from the necks of newborns
planting mint in back yards between
      cement cracks
wrapping sage and rosemary
      in lavender wind
kneading clouds into garlic to
cleanse confusion from our tongues

When we have let all the light
      into the temple
and unraveled the wisdom knots
you left in our pockets
then we will wear sunrise on our wrists
      instead of watches
know the wind as your breath
stirring us to
take the lessons out of notebooks
braid consistency into our nostril hair.
and to be present.

We are the children of
your emptiness and your fulfillment
challenged now
to weave the elder fabric
with threads of self.
Mark what we live
in the name of our queen mothers
Mark what we live
in the name of our queen mothers
who have stepped out.

RENEE SIMMS

THE DEATH OF SOUL

My first love did not come for me
On horseback, that was impractical.
Too much concrete on my block.
Too noisy for a horse, as well—
The tambourine shakes, doo-wop harmony &
In every other house lived slick, pretty
Men who could sing.
So he rode the FM airwaves, instead,
Guitar riffs on his tongue.
We were post-Motown but miracles
& temptations still lingered in
Our men with bass guitar voices
Our men who built pyramid homes. Our men drove
Cadillacs glossed by the moon & all this magic made me
One peculiar girl.

                        *

On our first date my love handed me
The center of a flower, no petals.
"Seduction is a principle," he said &
Because he was royalty, I believed.
Pamela's daddy, who sang backup, did not like him.
"Pornographic," her daddy said, "The devil," Mama would say
But what did they know? Pam's daddy had
Mistresses as vacant as Smokey's house
& Motown was dead at the edge of a continent,
The pious heel-spins by suited men
Cliches we no longer used.
I tape recorded my lover's songs,
Sketched his impish face upon schoolbooks.
One night I cried to him about the future
& he cupped my face inside his purple hands.
It was 1977.

"Nothing is permanent," he whispered,

"Not neighborhoods or soul music,"
Then my street went quiet as catholics &
All the dark, polished men were gone.

BELLE ISLE

(FOR DELETHA WORD)

Through the window of a yacht club
is a bride. She does not feel beautiful
although her makeup is exquisite, a
peacock's tail upon her face.

As a girl, she watched her mother paint herself
lovely each morning, at the kitchen table,
using one round, drugstore mirror and
tubes of browns and reds.

Today her mother looks plain by comparison
and busies herself by touching lipstick on the
cheek of each guest at the party.

Every face smiles, since

no one can know tomorrow—
a daughter becoming her mother,
the death of an uncle, an aunt's illness.

The loss of a breast. Jail and its profane
erasure of your soul.

Today is today
full of kisses and wine
brown hands brushing the hem of organza.

To know the family's misery you must notice
the grandmother's hands, the rivers for veins
and floorboard knuckles
or see that those in attendance laugh a little too much
or that after the *Amen*, the bar.

To know the city's misery
understand that where they gather is
Belle Isle, a place once covered with rattlesnakes
though lately it is broken glass.

That on the island the Saturday before this wedding
young people witnessed a woman's beating
then watched her arch as if on a low table and
dive naked into the river

But today is today, full of kisses and wine,
the bride's mother always with a glass,
the bride, drunk herself, repeatedly falls
but hands are swift to raise her up.

The father, a quiet man of numbers
jitterbugs as if on fire
and soul records play louder and faster,
throwbacks that remind everyone of days
without blight, days when singers and songwriters

danced at weddings, went to ballgames,
the city-blocks crammed with teachers living
next to musicians who knew mechanics
who married doctors

ROMUS SIMPSON

ON OUR 6ᵀᴴ ANNIVERSARY

it was nothing i have said
or have done
not a fine point of diplomacy missed the ritual banter
or the gulf between the cultures we merged in matrimony
not the shape of my thighs
the casual invitation of my belly
or the midnights your skin sang calypso
and you could not turn into me because some
woman downtown refused you
not the long november with its mathematics of falling leaves and
hemispheres of late stars
the hunger between them and the earth
not the talk left on the table and in the halls
and the rooms flowering beautiful cordial shadows
indifferent morning rising in the storm everywhere
nor the silence where the seed heart floats in a dark current
away from birth and possibility
that makes me remember my parents
makes me watch you asleep alone and unclaimed
in a tropical dark blue continent sailing
lost in some other sister's lush dream eye
who bears you children and sends them running to greet you
like my father who became immaculate
in being a machine at goodyear and moved each day
click by click tire by tire alarm by alarm toward a great tolling death
ahem by ahem until the lungs were a thick dry tongue
and left unkissed into the wide cold morning eternity
it was not the highlights in my hair
changing evening in my eyes
uncounted and not alive
rain from my sky and eyes on easter island
tongue touch to no one
the world a placid soundless ocean
and no map to find me in all this blue
and it is not the uncertainty of the mornings

when you walk out the door unasked
and you become my neighbor who works all week
then fishes on weekends and sleeps early
and i become his wife who has come to love her garden
because her home does not grow

AND THEY SAT THERE WAITING

so he was a man without a car
frugal and inexact as
the reality of bus schedules
and he was wearing an old tee shirt
something about california on it
small holes fretting near the collar
the worn sleeve about to tassle and sing
and his nameless jeans generic as
the day the pedestrians the vendors
and the requisite calico of loitering faces
the volume of her hair
pulled over her shoulder
like she was waiting for a lover
to come and kiss her
as if he had said "wait here, baby/don't move baby"
and had run to get the phone
and she did what he said
stood at the mirror how he wanted her
without error
feeling beautiful pushing her hips forward
trying not to be forward
but wanting so much
she looked soft as
a memory of water and dusk
made me think of diego rivera
how would he see her?
would she be the queen of a country
a revolution spinning and cursing toward her
would there be songs about her?
mariachis on the verge of tears
her dark eyes looking inward at a private sky
maybe, if diego rivera rode busses in los angeles
and saw her waiting with the world in fresco behind her
but no
her country is this bus depot
and the few unkempt streets leading here
these transportation commission tile murals
the freeway exchanges and their shadows
weeds that conquer concrete
and extend toward god

her memory someplace a language ago
coming north to this impersonal country
this country without festivals
and the male next to her said something
she looked up and smiled
he let a leg sprawl out
then tucked it back in
she followed his story
laughed
nudged his shoulder and
he came back laughing
and they sat there waiting
a coke between them
the day adrift in the world
like a rumor of sleep
the long gasoline afternoon
its hemispheres of clear windows
beyond the city in sifting panes of sun
everything north bright into the sky
somewhere out there in
the lull of an alley
the ornate quiet of roses
blooming in the grate of chainlink fences
before the cans are collected
and the rattle of the cart
presses the day back into sound
at the gentle hand of jazz
a jet searching the ionosphere
glints into the subconscious
they were waiting
he picked up the soda and drank
it was strong
and when he was through
she did the same
he continued to talk
evenly like an early catholic guitar
she turned her face full to see him
as if he was the only thing flowering in the world
was the coke his or hers?
they both seemed content
busses occasionally
filling the structure with sound

i read their advertisements
i watched their wheels turn
oh, the beautiful leaning of busses
it was my thirst wondering vaguely
a memory i carry of water and august
his spanish slowed looking at her
she was beautiful
i saw it too and was lost
he reached and touched her hair
she let him
and smiled
closed her eyes
and smiled
and let him
his face was gentle
no malice anywhere for miles
he touched her again and she remained
authenticated and round
as when the sun god ra
seeing the world was barren
touched earth and became all things
he touched her and became constituent to
the warm ripe country of her young body
and in the disappearance of the transit mall
he touched her again
lingered at her chin
i thought he would lean
and kiss her full
then recline wealthy
chanting speaking in tongues
dreaming of fruit
but he lingered respectfully
a city at the edge of the ocean
soon the starling will be rising
moving toward the early moon
hours now since that couple gathered their things
and boarded a city bus
no more opera busses going back out into the sun
only shadows now and the thinning day
more blue than earth now
an occasional hurrying someone
too far away to call to

the custodians are beginning their business
as the last of the busses turn into port
one bus blues
one bus mauves and oranges
then a quiet bus of stars

RAAKI SOLOMON

TEARS OF A CUPID

I introduced you two
Took a share in your joy
All up in the wedding cake
Smiles and pictures, now I got
A piece of the tears. I saw the glow
Of the baby in your face.
Bob Marley, said it all, "Every time I plant

A seed, he'd say, kill them before they grow
I shot the sheriff." Justice miscarries pain
Your stomach's stop, my bear, regret.
I am integral to remorse a cupid
Whose tears don't reach would be Mother.
Blank look groans of not a daddy

Empty stares to fire A bullet
No earthquake shifts the aching targets.
Kill time, wipe the blood
With pieces of our hearts.
Paint a picture, jog in the evening
Get lost in a public park. Greet

Family and friends who still stand.
We will kill clock till we have
No more tears to share....

HANNIBAL TABU

AS YET UNTITLED

Born from the belly of a loud-ass, redbone bayou woman,
you stand firm on the foundation of yourself
demand I let go tedious thoughts and be god.
Never afraid to get mad and ask me,
"Do you know magic?
Can you utter the name of your soul and bring yourself back to light?"
To be in your presence, I must emerge unblemished from valleys of
bat-wielding yesterdays.
To be worthy of your touch, need to recite your mantras in twelve tongues.
I am a man longing to attend perfection.

Rub my shoulders with savior's hands.
Align me between your wings, teach me all the levels of your identity.
No shame drinking in your round the way curves.
See, you delivered me from ladies of carnelian soul,
rescued me from anxious nights, kisses of poison and infidelity.
It's you that balances my heavy scales.
I am a man longing for synchronicity.

The way to win you can't be found on web pages or in Sun Tzu ...
it is written in the language of sacrifice.
Carved in forgotten runes along the bones of the left side of my body.
Teach me to remember.
Educate me so I can know your ways like I know my name.
When you open those apricot lips to cry out, I'll already be on guard.
Let you be when you retreat to my recliner,
wire glasses on ball of your nose, some book giving you a
wall to think behind.
Then, when you lay quietly, and sunlight treads lightly across your cheeks,
I'll smooth the strain from your waterfall crown of hair
and Stevie Wonder love you into rhapsody.
I, too, am a soul opening into light.

CRUSADER

Her quest for one flawless example of majesty
called out over sidewalks covered with
jagged footsteps and shimmers of line noise.

But I ain't no king, I'm a warlord,
protected by crumpled chestplate of inverted awe
Spray bottle of "git right" hangin' from my belt.

Asked me if I could replenish her faith in brothers,
but found war and hope chests were bare.
Boulevards of broken dreams
lie behind facade of my button-downed battlements.

All I have to offer
is a relentless embrace of right now,
terrified resolve to walk towards fear
because I'm bigger than apprehension ...

... even if I don't know it yet.

DEDICATION

This is not for the thugs.

This is for tired security guards catching the bus home, southbound on
Vermont.
This is for wire-rimmed web programmers dodging layoffs,
slumping when they stand, so people panic less when they walk in.

This is for liquor store managers with southern accents,
sixteen-year-olds with comic books tucked in back packs,
freelance reporters in denim button shirts and
the suited publicists who appreciate them more than either can say.

For labor-drenched customer service reps,
averting their eyes when a curvy backside sashays by,
knowing their woman's waiting at home.
For fifty-year-old brothers watching college ball on Saturday,
a recliner, the throne they can afford.

'Cause nobody writes shit for you.

This is not for the hoes.

No part of this is aimed at golddiggers,
or airbrushed vixens on video screens.

This is for overweight nurses with carpal tunnel syndrome,
everyday women dividing worry
between daughter at home and son who moved away.
Round the way hairstylists with good intentions,
sweetheart sisters who never dated a football player,
or a gangster,
or a pimp,
but always wanted someone special to love.

For Rosa Parks girls standing on windy corners,
stoically stationed at curb because nobody offered a seat on the bench,
off-duty waitresses swaying slowly to Mary J. Blige,
waiting for they man to put down the headset and answer her call,
as soon as he gets home.

Yeah, this is for the sisters you should marry,
not the ones you'll never get to date,
since nobody remembers them in story and song.

Let's hear it for those brothers.
Take a moment for them ladies,
diamond dedication in a zirconium world.

JERVEY TERVALON

GREEN HEAVEN

Ready for rolling hills
Sun warm on my face
the salt spray, walk the bluffs see
the raging surf.
think about what could have been
alizee

Moment of rapture
my rapture comes cheap
for the price of a tank of gas
the 101 runs through my life

See Atascadro
What goes on there?
Paso Robles
Maybe Martha lives there
Hilary I'm sure moved to Milpitas

Gina rides alongside me now
with baby Giselle
We listen to Al Green
and we are in Heaven

REMEMBERING EBONY AND MYIṢHA

Stevie says that God is inside
and it's taking him so long because we have so far to come
Maybe so,
two little girls left alone in Fresno's oven
Sure could have used an angel or two
to lift them up to bathe in cool streams.

Define tragic, see their faces.

LYNNE THOMPSON

SONG FOR TWO IMMIGRANTS

I thought I knew you. To me, you were the Grenadines,
the Anglican Church and a cricket match every Sunday
and every Sunday, you were Fort Charlotter, the Vincy Mas
and blue tidepools. You were Arawaks sailing into Kingston
Harbor. You were English and French patois, rainforests,
Regatta and a Congo snake, whelk, rotis, lobster and rum.

Yet, here you are in a yellowing photograph, snapped
in the Mojave or Death Valley, CA, looking like deserters
from an American war: her, every bit the boy hair slicked,
leather jacket cinched at her throat, one tiny foot on the running board of a black `37 Ford coupe and you, looking
nothing less than the black Clyde Barrow, flicking the butt
of your Lucky Strike while checking out your boys playing
in the dirt, wearing shortpants and high-tops, everyone looking
for all the world as if the Caribbean were a dream, a far yesterday away, and it was, and it's clear that I did not know you.

THE HOUSE OF MANY PLEASURES

(INSPIRED BY BILL PAJAUDA'S RAMPART STREET LADIES)

It never matters what time it is in Rampart's House of Many Pleasures
because it's always the hour of incense, the hour of bourbon and no-goods.

In the violet dusk, some cool papas with coin are always sniffing after us
begging us to low-tone their bugles, to slide their water keys, to shake our
castanets.

In the scarlet a.m., some used-to-be somebody's mama always shows up
asking after her Tom, Dick or Harry, all the while memorizing the scent of
our brass.

But we're no dimuendoes and we cannot be riffed. There is no other, no
Skylark nor Sweet Lorraine. We're the blues the world forgets when we lie
between a man's thighs,

perfume of sin and reefer bleeding from our fingertips. We are wildcats for a
sweet daddy. We bite when you beg us to. Here, in this Sidney Bechet dark,
this fugue

for the hardcore, we slide bronze and wet from Louis' horn at half-past
dreams in this House of lethal delights where you tell us your tawdry secrets
just past the hour of desire,

no matter what time the violet dusk, the scarlet a.m., where we taste of
cinnamon, taste of clove, about the time that we surrender, about the time we
slide you down, slow

MUDCLOTH

it was you outside of the poetry reading
last wednesday night
you at the doorway
and although i was self conscious and paying attention
when i saw you there
baby tied to your chest
with mudcloth, with care
i opened the door
i let you in
two big headed brown smiling faces

i had been calling you
you had been calling me
feeling call, spirit call
the way old lovers communicate
when phones are complicated, forbidden

i was prouder the other night
of you as i have ever been
cause when all the soft knotted sisters
cooed when you walked in the door so careful
and you eased your lovely package in mudcloth
i remembered when i was with you
remembered how fine it was
when we were at our best
when it was a sunny, dusty l.a.
at the african marketplace
when our bracelets chimed our footsteps
like petals from raining spring trees
we, in joy, in mystery
as we blessed each other
anointed our locks with frankincense
making pungent crosses on our foreheads
before work, after church
baptizing me at the lip of venice

our locks filled with sea foam and jesus

mornings with you were always my favorite
waking me up early, baby
and sweet in the morning

scriptures in the tape deck
instant coffee and heavy cream
clove cigarettes

and mudcloth on the wall
a pleasantly brown bible study, us two
and me, finding jesus
you shaping savior for me
in the palms of your beautiful hands

i broke all the rules
at my afrocentric school
believing in the greatest story every told
i held the secret between my breasts
in my cheeks, the soles of my feet
like light bulbs
like christmas
still do

donny hathaway and oranges
made me cry last night when i thought of you
as i ate the fruit
something about the sweet readiness
to satisfy, to nourish
is so opposite of what we became
and donny knew it
saying goodbye to us
now, when it is hardest

it might be wrong
but when i saw the dimples
on your son's cheeks
i thought of how much you wanted him
how you called him

while making love to me
he had a name before even a story
how you frightened me
how unready i was to accept the gift
stripes on my belly
a promise forever
how you frightened me

but when i saw him there
each cheek permanently embracing a kiss
i felt he was a little bit of me
and wasn't he there
when we tried to work it out
when we came undone
when she loomed like a fertile moon
leaving no time for healing or second questions
saying i miss you
is too small
saying goodbye is impossible

believe me, this life is harder
without your encouragement, baby
harder without sweet wakening
to you whispering prayers over my dreams

life is harder without your lusty affirmation of my body
there was a time you loved my pliant and full brown more than i
i take better care of myself now
sweeter, probably sweeter than you remember

they say mudcloth is used for shrouds
for goodbye
but i say mudcloth is for beginnings
for soft soaking of frankensence
tears and sweet babies

and love, love is the color brown
find our story on a few yards of fabric
in the hood somewhere

notice the soil finger painting
of how we found each other

how we loved
how we forever stained a story
we are still telling

THE FIRE THIS TIME. REMEMBERING APRIL 1992

i remember saying
boo
to a volvo on the westside
filled with frightened white faces

who was i to be afraid of, anyway
a 20 something, veggie, westside girl
fighting the good fight of inclusion and voice
at a predominately white community college by the beach
where my best friends sold jewelry and fell in love

boo
and i became their worst fear
and what must that fear look like
a skirt made of watermelon rinds
my face blackened with coal
each braid secured with tiny little white bows
my head tilted to one questioning angle

uga, booga, booga boo

and i am the mistral show
the kill whitey nightmares are made of
the organizing, uppity type
the well read new negro with all the answers

a revolution over my right shoulder
an army of fatigued nappy babies in black berets to my left
and my man, my king
festooned in armory of red, black and green
kwanzaa baskets rimming with fruit and ears of corn
habari gani, my sister
as my brown fist eclipses all traces of light

i am none of those things
you won't find me hiding underneath a yard of fabric
with charcoaled eyes waiting for my turn to speak

you won't find me
yelling sister soldja style
getting my point across with a reverberating mic
at a rally somewhere downtown

let me explain:

i know what it's like to be called nigger
to favor the fairer without knowing why
to fold my lips inward, suck them smaller than they are

i remember fresh permanent relaxers
and leaving the salon
a southland breeze feathering all the shiny, scabbed crown of me
as i got in the car and sang songs on the wrong side of the f.m. dial
remembering the anorexic, ditto and candies clad white girls of hale jr. high
who taught me how to hate my body

see this rage comes from somewhere
i remember finding out about the harlem renaissance
at a bookstore on the westside
all big and glossy

like, of course you know about these painters and posers for james van der
zee
of course you marveled at the way he captured light on smoke and bourgeois
ladies
how he made up allegories with children superimposed in wedding portraits
and angels in still lifes of the dead

there is a scream that occurs when you are left out of something
a dying happens
to blacks who don't want you to acknowledge them at a westside gathering
the dread who favors the white girls
the way candy flavors sweet
i mean without one, there is no other

there is a place where silence comes from
i remember tanks on palms boulevard
counting the flame twisters of south central
the day we learned our lives were cheaper than we suspected

all i wanted to do
was to make sure my brother was safe
and that my mama got home from the valley
that we were together
that we could survive this
praying that it would pass
and hearing over and over
that quote from a place i have forgotten

      you know you will be ready for a revolution
      when you are ready to eat rats

the grocery store on the corner
sold out of every bag of bread and gallon of milk
we watched newscasters all us names, finding a place for their rage
we watched interviewers on tv
asking the poor why they were taking baby formula and diapers
from abandoned markets
i suppose i never felt so small
so silent
because i wasn't ready for no bloody revolution
wasn't ready to eat rats
and the fist i held up on la brea and wilshire that first night
was to protect myself from a brother standing in the middle of the street
looking for a place to put his bullets, his rage

i do what i am supposed to
learn to look beyond the signifiers of class and color
understand that beyond every revolution
is another story, another oppression

one summer in south central on a schoolyard
i noticed that everyone was brown
each african, cambodian, chicano child
looked a bit like me
i couldn't make out their races as they played
and i realized that we shared something that i couldn't exactly name

it is that same feeling i get
when my friend jeff
writes an enlightened poem
about the violation of white privilege

and owns his own peculiar benefit dolled by the slave trade, centuries ago

it will be impossible to pay the debt
to rub smooth the relief of slavery from our backs
there may always be a time

when we favor our hair as smooth and glassy as michael jackson's
look at the toll colonization and self-hatred has taken on his face
i believe in love
and i will believe in it
until i am gone
until my scars are ash
and i am the sum of my journals

besides
how are you gonna hold hands with anyone
with your fists all balled up like that

A.K. TONEY

WORLD STAGE PERFORMANCE GALLERY
(FOR BILLY HIGGINS AND HORACE TAPSCOTT)

Where every witness is ascending more into feeling
the I was born from voice melodizing praise
to learn expression ancestors created...
music is church washed in red bleeding
on walls of communion fully breaded
vine flows a wine of life, influential spirits hang
and every noise is a message waiting to be
heard... let healing begin...

Art not word for testimony?
For truth is resulted through soundlightprint...
medium where pulpit is raised and uplifted...
only stand of notes with proverbial psalm.

holy space all worlds spin scripture carved in foundation...
sermon felt Billy ride his stik in us and make house jump...
felt Horace chords harp avant-garde exotic
plucks in blak and wite keys opening doors.
Sanctuary where griot rhythm mated.

O' GREAT NEGUS

(FOR RICHARD FULTON OF 5TH STREET DICK'S COFFEE COMPANY)

O' Great Negus
Calling all Souljahs!
O' Great Negus
Roots and Wordsmiths!
O' Great Negus
O' Great, O' Great

O' Shadym was a great nigga along with
his brother Jaheed providing a new temple
of Wordsmith... It is believed they apprenticed
underneath an elder known to the roots as Ras Richard

It was when grey twists slowly but surely lock
and sparks shot from the burning bush as doja
from the biblical encyclopedia... For like a wound
inflames a finger, such is a thought that inflames
the mind... and great sunburnt people proverb
words of molten melting magnificence liquiefying
soil into sand transforming transparency wild rooting
in rude boy stylie... foundating fertility
to follow and flow, follow and flow
water to soul and spirits hear it,
and spirits hear it...

O' Great Negus
O' Great, O' Great
O' Great Negus
O' Great, O' Great

And King to Queen in chek-mate...
what color r the sands of the son? Are they melanin of
golden brown and bronze?
O' a sweet brown lady, right... fled the fool to tongue tie
a tool and speak of cool conspiracy... for Khefri...
Yr High Pimpstress dreaming dark skin gleaming
from inside surface

Shock the monkeys, like the birds of fowl
blooming follicle flower from her natural smooth
pelvic pose...
O' pregnant moon!
O' pregnant moon on orgasmic alert ovulating the stars
waiting for halo as Snake Doctor charms wife
with kemetic clouds of light
cosmic eclectic life...
into photon aeons beyond ray years ago...
she is power, she is poem
she is power, she is poem
and human subjects r but pets in presence
of her High Pimpstress...
For Earth is the root, and the root is the Earth

O' Great Negus
O' Great Negus
O' Great Negus

O' great nigga of justice can be sacrificed
scare scarred for life... Once upon a one
time enemy Brother Norm "Nomzee" Maxwell
disturbed the peace by exposing dollar
signs on a paper cloth... I'm talking about
the dead devils with the cain green eye
atop of pyramids, straight narrow paths with
the curly reptiles going through the middle
while Blak Gods pray by chanting...
O' Mister Dow Jones!
O' Mister Dow Jones!
O' Massa, O' Massa!
O' Massa, the dollar made me do it!..
The Dollar made me do it!
Ole Massa pulverizing the mass of minds
like a penis poking for a piece of asphault
the Hill and Street blus was built on corrupt
when blood erupts from our stomachs
vomit from deformed downers
third eyes spying through nipples
trying to filter a dance in the 5th dimension
while demons doubt a dying species to exist
and flesh is their greatest wish...

while demons doubt a dying species to exist
and flesh is their greatest wish...

O' bump me big blak bodacious booty and blow...
O' bump me big blak bodacious booty and blow and blow
the aura of turnips from a boombox blasting...

let the bidding begin...
let it start at 1-150...
can i get 2?...
We have 3- 500
Do i have 1?
1500 from the gentle of macadocious in the back...
Can I get 2 for this fine speciman of slang
blak from the botom of the sea, pick of the b-o-n-e
2500 from the guy with the goosed down feathered word
Can I get 3 or 4 for the 5th Street Dick's Coffee Cart
crak from the back of an addict slave whom became
a Negus, a Blak King
5000 from the the Blak Queen sheen skin with purple
can I get 10,15,20,30,40,50,
Ladies and Gentleman,
do I have the mythical, magical, spiritual power
more than 100 million of us jumped for free...
Poets r still humming the hymn...

O' Great Negus
O' Great Negus
O' Great Negus
O' Great Negus
O' Great Negus,
O' Great, O' Great
O' Great, O' Great
O' Great Negus...

It was Shango in the sky, Lava rock who was his Father
Pedro Ajamu keeps flame of hip-hop burning in sweat lodge
Teach of humbleness to receieve blessing from White Eagle
Phoenix singing
Dragon roaring
Visions breathing

Phoenix singing
Dragon roaring
Visions breathing
iris of creation, born in cremation
iris of creation, borin in cremation
the secrets, the iris
the iris, the secrets
the secrets of wordsmith in foundation
never ever tire inside the Great Negus
Wordsmith and Roots Empire...

O' Great Negus
Calling all Souljahs!
O' Great Negus
Roots and Wordsmith!
O' Great Negus
O' Great, O' Great

DEBRA A. VARNADO

AN L. A. RHYTHM

Dragging shopping carts,
Mountains of dirty laundry, sleeping babies.
Running for the RTD bus
That morphed into the MTA
And sometimes never stops, arrives on time, or delivers.
Feeling the tug of sex in a sleepy groin.
Husband is huddled on the corner
At the hardware store, looking for a day's work,

Finding a whore's self in front of his face.
He needs some self, but not that one.
He blows her off at predawn,
His cigarette smoke-- the freshest breeze of her day.
With his buddies, on their haunches.
Leaning on walls, half-brick, half-cast iron,
Day sheds its darkened halo,
Morning glistens over the roof of the laundromat.

The baby, he is in dream, wants his Mother.
Softness of an inner arm,
The curve of a breast, a nipple to hold.
But she sways this way and back on a bus.
Feeling the rhythm that comes and goes.
In real time, Broadway to Fifth,
Transfer, two down, one to go,
Food 4 Less, Hope then Spring.

PAM WARD

JEREMY STROHMEYER

When the devil checked
into the Primadonna
he had on a
baseball cap
some nike shorts
a nasty-ass T-shirt
with both nipples pierced
which he showed
to the whole hotel crew.
Checked in under the name Strohmeyer
and strolled straight
to the arcade.
Had a poker face
a handful of nickels
and a filthy mind.
Eyed the black girl
playing alone
like last night's meat.
Fed her coin after coin
lifted her to the machine.
See, the devil was so helpful
had that cherry coke grin
hiding rotten capped teeth
copped a couple of gin and tonics
and was well on his way
to that fake I.D. high
he felt good
he felt free
like that first sight of Vegas
in the black desert night
like the dice rolling nothing but sevens.
the girl was so glad
to have someone to play
there was hide-n-go seek
and patty-cake too

they laughed all the way into the bathroom
I ain't lying
cuz the handicap sign saw
the whole bloody thing
those fingers
those clothes ripped
and thrown to the floor
her scream smothered
shut in his lap.
He sat on her
smashed both her feet
in that bowl
held her whole body
down in that wet filthy grave
that white porcelain tomb
oh, the paper towels cried
couldn't take anymore
the Wash your Hands sign looked away
But ol' Strohmeyer sat
still as death
didn't move
watching ol' ladies
walking back in and back out
snapped that young black girl's neck
like some folks slap their cards
snapped it twice
he said,
"just to make sure"

See, this is an ugly poem
this is a poem for parents who
gamble on faith
leave their babies outside
left like big plates of food
like a dog pan
a bone
any ol' hound can sniff
leave them playing alone
and their only defense
is a roomkey, a coke and a dime
see this poem is a prayer
this poem says beware

be alert cuz the devil's nearby
always hunting for food
always looking for you or your
wandering tots
got a pocket just jangling
a stack of trick cards
a white icepick smile
and a criminal mind
a nailfile and thick jagged teeth

(Dedicated to Sherrice Iverson, Enis Cosby, the Atlanta Children and all
those who never saw him coming.)

PAPERPLATES

the good ol' days then
were late nights in the kitchen
canned beans and weenies
and fries cooked in fat
war food that talked back
and thrashed in hot grease
and popped if you got up too close
but we loved it
loved standing there
right next to mom
near the comforting warmth
of her house dress
we stood watching hotdogs
exploding like welts do
gruesome skin oozing with juice
near the flame
near her elbow
we stood there
in peace
and the quiet
of daddy's not home yet.

CAR FIGHT 59

I like LA, particularly
the car racing in residential areas.
The last one was with this obnoxious slob
in a white gloss benz.
Cut me off big time.
Him and his fat cigar
barbie bitch
glued to his lap.
Passed me with one hand.
I had to brake so hard
my groceries wrecked
the backseat.
It really pissed me off
but I got back next to em
and blasted the most
ghetto rap tape I had.
Slide all the windows down
and started bobbing too
like I gave a fuck
acting oblivious
to his dog-faced mug
and stuck-up date.
I waited in the right lane
foot hovering the gas
like a crook
ready to smashed it down
the second that sucker went green.
Wasn't even where I wanted to go.
But sometimes you gotta show folks
let em know that
we all own these streets
even if it means
taking in extra scenery.

Conney D. Williams

HOUSE PARTY

honey coated black teenagers
conjuring SWEET tabasco magic
Friday nights transforming hungry adolescence
into SHAFT, SUPERFLY and FOXY BROWN
via platform shoes,
double knit bell-bottom pants
mini-skirts,
blow-out kits
black lights
"hey, ain't that bobby womack?"
the music leaking from the house was a compass
gave aching bodies direction
with each elongated step
drowned us with anticipation
the lush taste of ebony desire
like big mama on front porch
rocking in favorite chair, steady
lemonade always within arm's reach
the desire to touch this underage immortality
caused salivating hearts to hasten
earnest's mom had just bought that wall-to-wall stereo
45's was stacked in rotation and dropping
cheap diamond needle scratching vinyl
we didn't know better...didn't care
we wanted was to hear that music
putting dents in our backs
creating lather between legs
it gave meaning to our everyday
we always got a daily dose of soul
this night was no exception
pre-adult perspiration dropped
like summer rain upon the doorway
no escape from the sugary thickness inside
a living room of congealed funk
alive and clinging

to our bodies like maple syrup
poured from mouth of a mason jar
smelling like sweet sticky sex
each participant trying to catch their breath
sparks fly even with the lack of oxygen
stars litter skies smeared with indelible ink
hot night in a louisiana summer
brimming with youthful possibility
never many sightings in our neighborhood
i saw few escape the reign of despair
existing within the boundaries
of shreveport's city limits,
but this was an extraordinary nights
when a young black southern boy
not only realized his doubted sexuality
but caught a vision beyond life's axis
keeping time at corner of long and doris streets
weekend recess from chores and academic
caught me and my boys concentrating
on one thing able to
elude despair of mooretown
so, me, lee arthur and luther
followed the fresh scent of female adolescence
along tarred streets and shortcuts through yard
back of mr. polo's store and duplex
faces stained with hai karate
back pockets filled with miniature liquor bottles
five finger discounted from walgreens
so we could party in our right mind
almost impossible to unearth acceptance
when you're the smart kid
and i was a ruddy runt
already knew too much at sixteen
filled with hometown naivete
a dollar short of self appreciation
i existed on the hope of change
lived vicariously through teenage exploits of others
it seemed an eternity
before I finally grew more than just inches
and found courage to know "real" cool
lee arthur was my idol and best friend
young girls called us "cat eyes"

but he was a prince among commoners
a sinewy jock with three sports letters
hair parted off center and a driver's license
never told him he was my hero
even though I never understood
why he quit the football team senior year
luther was court jester,
ghetto comedian
illiterate and dark as coal
and native american cheekbones
he had a way of settling disputes
via fist diplomacy
that always quieted adversaries
kicked my ass a few times
but he always had my back
hard to believe teenie weenie's dad
emptied a gun into him over change for a ten
forgot to tell him that I loved him
viet nam was finally closing shop
anti-black schools integrated
while the beatles insisted we "let it be"
yet, all the world i ever wanted to know
was inside that front door
mixture of sweat and funk percolating
gladiators of groove with bodies clashing
tearing away the amour of inhibitions
the beat undulated the crowd
hypnotizing us with each note
pounding rhythms into our spine
there was pam boyd tucked in a dim kitchen corner
my seventh grade crush all grown up
but puberty never granted me courage
to approach her beauty
the dance floor was a jehovah witness recruiter
drafting every person
who was willing to open its door
then suck them into a black hole of funk
each melody insisted we stomp our feet
beneath al green moans
temptations' harmonies
they created an urban earthquake
GOD must have created house parties

day after he showed eve to adam
arms flailing,
backs arched
asses in flight
earthbound angels reaching for something divine
"distant lover" manifests life in the form of slow drags
hard-ons grow from close encounters
girls thighs part like red sea
at rising of each young moses' staff
grinding is the teenage prayer
bennie ray has carrie mae
slipping into darkness
wishing curfew was midnight
'stead of leb'n thirty
confidence is manna to youthful tongues
cause phone numbers to rain from eight-foot ceilings
marvin's preaching bring confessions
to dance floor altar calls, and a
stove top kiss got me thinking I'm chosen
but, i'm still two virgin summers shy
of self confirmation

SISTAS (I LIKE IT)

too much black life been defined by jamestown
and serena williams, she u.s. open
a cat suit in a dog's season
lycra lean, girl got back
back like pre-american history
like all them white country clubs
where she practices dissimilation
pouncing on unsuspecting debutantes
dispatching them like private tennis lessons
she don't really fit in
but she got access and assets
ass kickings reside in her forehand
they envy her game,
that chiseled onyx frame
jealousy has many aliases
like them television images that feign acceptance
glaring with a precision ugly
even at grand slam tennis tournaments
and serena, she ghetto fab
tall drink of compton cocoa
blonde too, but she ain't no heather
no anna kournikova
she done already won this game,
ain't waiting no return from vogue or cosmopolitan
to emaciate her self-esteem
or mold her into a european model of beauty with bilemic backhands
cause serena she thick
thick like sistas sposed to be
thick lips, thick eyes
thick hips, thick thighs
mostly a thick attitude
(and i like it)
think she done realized
acceptance only gots to be on your terms
racism like lycra if you wear it long enough
stretching like rope to lynch any cultural references
or attempts to express gratitude
for features AFRICAN
to flow the way the Niger run

natural hair and shapes are held in contempt
lacks loveliness unless given massa's approval
even some of us buy into that shit
with self deprecation, michael jackson and permanents
like joyce brothers hypothesizing
incapable of realizing
that white men, they fantasize
bout sistas with question marks
attached at the base of their backs
they just don't want white psychologists
to include it in their research
recognize service has been broken
it's century 21 and your volleys fall short
sexy ain't an exclamation point
in a white tennis dress
it ain't barbie, london or new york fashion
it ain't net working depictions
hollywood fiction or restrictions
on screen castrations
or the limitation of black men in love scenes
but that's another script
season's changed to fall
one size does not fit all
big bone-ded is a turn on
full lips sucking my tongue
the chocolate, the honey, the brown sugar
(and i like it)
whenever success isn't transparent and wears color
roaches come out
to infest the environment
with another anorexic super model
trying to roast our futures in easy bake ovens
and cookie cutter images of attractive
but my view is from another definition
standards that exceed your perception
the queen...the mother...the sista
giving birth to relentless beauty
celebratedly refined and altogether undefined
by your conditions and labels
no collagen needed
no implants necessary
because in the beginning

GOD took the dust and HE created
and SHE still exists and she is my desire
(and i like it)

ANGELO WILLIAMS

CASA-MAL-WAPHA

Aztlan prophecy
To fruition, in Tito
Riding down Crenshaw
In his Tacoma pick up
Playing "Banda" like "Boogie Down"
On twenty-two's.

Chicanisimo never counted on
The Guatemalans, y los Salvadorians, and the Nicaraguans
Who could care less for MechA.

These are Teddy Roosevelt's children
Who know no unity between el barrio and the ghetto
Only zero dollar down, 20 to a house, standing on Slauson waiting for more
work
& counting all the minutes between 1989 and right now
that it took Tito to get here
  to this car dealership.

Conspicuous consumption shines like red badge of courage
Surviving one war to get out of Managua
And another to get into Inglewood.

Manifest destiny
Never so dusty as
Old Californians coming back to establish a new Central
America.

The South won the War

Zapata's bones did not bury
The poor always look for bread
No moses through this mojave
NAFTA masquerades as manna
When all the while

it was an agreement to promote
slave wages

Sharecrop to this:
Elites "cousin up" on either side of the Rio Grande
Free trade agreements are a plan
For 21st century business men to experience
The feeling of being 18th century southern gentry
Mint Julip Mojito, salt the rim,
Body shots off these Zapatistas
"No, you can't put your lips on this,
they're just too thick
to speak Castilliano"

Where are all the Mexicans?

Where are all the Mexicans who wanted to be just like us?
Where are all the Mexicans who wanted to be Black?
Where is Oscar Gomez y Fast Eddie Salas whose falsetto freaked Smokey's
"Tears of a Clown" like Eddie was homegrown south central.

Where are the all the Mexicans who listened to our music in their lowriders
and didn't west side rolling Crip but sho nuff East Side 14th Street gang
banged?

Where are all the fine funny sad girls with 15 feet aqua net high hair with
them oblong shaped booties and damm you wanted to talk to her,
but you just couldn't do that,
you just couldn't do that
and she knew why
you just couldn't do that.

And Tito does not like Puerto Ricans
And Juanito does not like Tito
And Danillo y Ermelinda con los pello blanca
They just have preferences

"Angelo, trust, this is my culture and I'm telling you, they're just dirty
people."

Central Americans play Sicilians on Slauson waiting
Van Sertima sings Humpty: "All around the world it's the same song."

Olmec markers: nose tip to broad hip,
to brown skin the same white man's burden.

Winthrop Jordan rides shot gun as the dank foot odor in the six seater from
Pacoima to Encino to Orange County back to Slauson and Tito did that
seven days a week for 10 years

And when he met Danillo
And he was hanging with that kid Ricky
And they was selling that yellow crack rock
And he made $3,000 dollars in just one day
He could care less if Eugene got hooked,
sold his motorcycle, his T.V, his 1983 pearl white Ford truck with plush
leather seats, air conditioning, am/fm cassette player and cup holder

Had my momma out in the streets till midnight looking for him
Tito didn't care
Tito didn't know
Tito!

On twenty-two's.
Aztlan like King Alferd Plan
Riding down Crenshaw…
"Love is gonna get you, Love is gonna get you, Love is gonna get you. It's
gonna get-chu."

JAHA ZAINABU

MUSINGS

today i heard a gunshot in the alley under my window
i am not wise to the makes and sizes of guns
i am a poet, an artist, a mother

three shots to be precise
not just me
somebody else hadta heard it too
it is three in the afternoon a sunny day, june

these are the things that riot my headspace when i endeavour to write about
grandmothers, garvey, drums
my poems are little now
perhaps someones life has ended and no one has missed a beat

at the liquour store crazy melvin is begging for change
rolanda the crackhead is selling pussy
in unit b demarco is smoking weed
the couple downstairs is making love and i am listening because it is beautiful

i imagine she lays face downward and grips the headboard tightfisted
while he is stroking inside of her thick

the cushion of her backside is christmas rent paid

the fucking is good
i am never short of stories on buckingham rd
an elegant name for a street with such drama
even more ironic that it intersects king
yesterday someone pissed in the hallway

the ice cream truck comes by after dark
last october the brothas set of fireworks for two and a half hours starting at
one in the am
i would like to blame this on the white man
it is eleven pm and i am up writing because that is what i do

but i am in search of the who of who i am on this saturday night in los
angeles
where someone is being asked to dance
bishop collins is preparing his message
and good times dont come on local networks no more

maybe michael was too black too strong for tv
and thelma to georgous to be nappy and brownskinned
and i surmise they killed off james because white america couldnt handle a
black man
sticking with his family through bad times

i am writing
the musings and prophecies just come
wednesday before last the children were out front playing
there were two girls and a boy on one side and three girls on the other
a volleyball type game except there was one boy in the middle trying to get
the ball
in my day

i am old enough to have a day
we called it keep away now
monkey in the middle
this i believe i can blame on the white man
except there were no black mothers objecting to the madness

ive said it before and ill say it again
life in the hood aint always bad
like on fridays hank the dealer buys books and balloons and toys and food for
the children

who dont have very much
grandmamas and granddaddies are maams and sirs
and the piece and sage sistas are queens and miss ladies

but the splendor of moments like these and more are shadowed by my
neighbor claire
getting the fuck beat out of her by her boyfriend

i dont know his name but i am so sorry that i cannot make her have a better
life

every kick follows a stupid bitch this and every slap a silly muthafucka that
i am sorry

and through the tears my mind wanders
and i fancy leimert park recalled little africa where all the businesses are black
owned
for real

and the young sistas in training eagerly recieve council from the she elders on
hoochie coochie frying chicken and being grown

and the brothas are braided daishikied and employed

it is saturday night in the jungle and i am just
writing

EPILOGUE

The poems anthologized in "voices from leimert park: a poetry anthology" have spoken evenly, loudly, seductively, and oftentimes lovingly for themselves, with frequent eloquence, for, from and about Black Los Angeles, the razor blade of the Cutting Edge. Leimert Park, as much a state of being as a locale, has, since the nineties, become the de facto heart of a rich and welcoming cultural gathering, with The World Stage, its regulars and guest poets at the core. Each poet, in his or her fashion, has invited the reader into their artistic concerns, ideas and observations. We hope this assemblage has awakened or stirred a profound appreciation, for we are Western poets who also call ourselves Afro-, African-American, or just plain "Black" or just plain American, no matter the place of origin. Collections of literature from Los Angeles writers and poets, and from the southwest in general, are unfortunately rare occasions; however, when they appear, they summon considerable celebration, if considerable trepidation: Will "they" like us? Will "they" hear what we have to say? Have we represented ourselves well? These are questions we invite the enlightened reader to answer. What we celebrate and share amongst ourselves, and what we contribute to the whole of American and World literature, is the ceaseless courage to reverse the negatives that others use to define us:

We make poetry out of our negatives. We write poems that eat steak after midnight, poems that are drunk on and under the influence of love, that bump the gums and run the lips; poems so inspirational, you'll reach for your tambourine, so full of truth they'll split the pants off a lie, so sweet they have to be cut with salt. We write poems that break-and-enter the soul.

And on top of that, we reinvent the positives.

Given ALL OF THAT, it astonishes me that a new century has begun, and yet the lives and works of many of us remain invisible in our nation's literary spectrum. We hope this offering of "voices from leimert park: a poetry anthology" will brighten our presence with its light. In making this offering, know that it is done in the spirit of those who pioneered the west generations ago, taming its wildness, the griots dismissed as slaves, the word-musicians and word-warriors who were our literal and figurative ancestors. May these pages, with which we honor them, recharge, refresh, and re-inspire all who partake of these bold and blessed words for decades to come.

Wanda Coleman
Los Angeles

BIOGRAPHIES

Mikael Ahadou, born in 1958, attended Addis Ababa University and majored in Philosophy, after completing his third year he was imprisoned and tortured which resulted in the personal challenges he faced in later years. After his release he fled to the US through Djibouti in 1982. Ahadou has a B.A. in Literature from Cal State Dominguez Hills and was completing his Masters at the time of his death on May 2, 2003. In the last seven years, he held poetry workshops at Barber and Floyd Mental Health Clinic, as he believed poetry had been a salvation for his own challenges. Leimert Park was his refuge and sanctuary.

Riua Akinshegun, visual artist, writer and performance artist, has performed her poetry and stories for the Armand Hammer Museum, Mark Taper Forum, Writer's Guild of America as well as on international stages of Mexico, Guyana, and Suriname. Akinshegun has completed Market Bag, a family story. She is currently working on her autobiography, Home Grown.

Kim Benjamin is a mother of three, an educator and a poet, living, writing and praying in Los Angeles. She has been published in "The Supergirls Handbook: A Survival Guide," edited by Pam Ward.

Jennifer Bowen is a poet and actress native of St. Louis, MO. Jennifer has been featured on Tour with Erykah Badu and is the feature poet on several CDs.

Shonda Buchanan/Nyesha Khalfani, poet and journalist, is a fellow of the Sundance Institute, PEN Center USA West Emerging Voices and the California Community Foundation. An assistant professor of English at Hampton University, Shonda is currently editing a novel, a memoir, a collection of poetry and a novella.

Paul Calderon is a native of Los Angeles. His work has been featured in numerous venues and printed in various anthologies. He has a B.A. in Philosophy and M.F.A. in Film. His voice is an expression of a wide range of experiences ranging from late night Jazz jam sessions to his years of military service. Currently he is writing and directing for film and stage.

Wanda Coleman. Satire and the lyrical govern recent works by COLEMAN, known for her fierce observations and celebrations of life: *Ostinato Vamps* (Pitt Poetry Series 2003-2004), *Wanda Coleman's Greatest Hits: 1966-2003* (Pudding House, 2004), and *The Riot Inside Me: More Trials & Tremors* (David Godine, 2005).

Kamau Daáood, performance poet and community arts activist is a native of Los Angeles. He is the author of two chapbooks, *Ascension* and *Liberator of the Spirit*, and a widely acclaimed spoken word CD, *Leimert Park*, for which he received a PEN Oakland Award. He is also the subject of an award winning film, *Life is a Saxophone*. A former member of the Watts Writer's Workshop, Daáood honed his skill as a "word musician" for the Pan African People's Arkestra under the direction of pianist and composer Horace Tapscott. In 1989, he and master drummer Billy Higgins co-founded The World Stage in the Leimert Park area of Los Angeles, and under their leadership this storefront performance gallery became Los Angeles' black creative epicenter. In addition to numerous awards for his civic and artistic activities, Kamau Daáood has received a Cave Canem Workshop/Retreat Fellowship, a Durfee Artist Fellowship, as well as a California Arts Council Fellowship. He is the director of the performance group *An Army of Healers*, and to learn more visit: www.KamauDaáood.com.

Michael Datcher is the author of the New York Times Bestseller, *Raising Fences*, and also director literary programs at The World Stage Anansi Writers Workshop. He currently teaches at Loyola Marymount University.

Jawanza Dumisani is head of literary programming for The World Stage Anansi Writers Workshop in LA. He is also a 2004-2005 PEN Fellow and was an up and coming in the 2003 Los Angeles Poetry Festival. His first collection of poems called Stoetry was published on FarStarFire Press in March 2003.

Ruth Forman is the author of two award-winning books of poetry: *We Are The Young Magicians* and *Renaissance* (Beacon Press). She is currently completing her first novel, Mama John, and a third collection of poetry.

Peter J. Harris has published his poetry, personal essays, and articles since the 1970s. He's an editor, broadcaster, and arts educator. His book, *Hand Me My Griot's Clothes,* won the Josephine Miles Award.

LeVan D. Hawkins is a Los Angeles-based poet/writer/actor/performance artist. He is currently completing his first book of poems, "Autobiography of A Contradiction." Destiny.

Regina Higgins, resident of West Covina, California is a current volunteer for the World Stage Anansi Writers Workshop and a member of the National Federation of Chaparral Poets. She has been published in *The Messenger* and *The San Gabriel Valley Quarterly*.

Yuri Hinson, an LA native, is an irregular feature on the spoken word scene. She considers The World Stage's Anansi Writers Workshop her poetic birthing ground.

Jamal Holmes is from Los Angeles. He is a real nice guy with some kids and a wife.

Wendy James/Tcheconsase lives and writes in Los Angeles, California. Mother of a beautiful creative daughter, Wendy has performed her poetry throughout Los Angeles and published a collection of poetry.

Art Nixon thanks his son, Dr. Adilifu Nama, for getting him to write poetry again. Took "Pops" to Leimert Park, knowing that the level of so many writers there would knock him out...It sure did!!

V. Kali Nuriga is a mother and a writer, who raised three children, is raising two grandkids and still writing.

Jason Luckett is a singer-songwriter based in Los Angeles. His guitar laden groovy acoustic soul is a vibrant mixture of passion and peace. Influenced by Bob Dylan and Marvin Gaye, Luckett's sixth album, Mystery and Wonder, will be released in June 2005.

Josslyn Luckett lives in Los Angeles and writes everywhere, including a 2005 residency at Hedgebrook in Whidbey Island, Washington and most summers in San Antonio, Texas as a member of the Macondo Workshop founded by Sandra Cisneros.

K. Curtis Lyle was born and raised in Los Angeles, California. He was a founding member of the Watts Writers Workshop, joining in 1966 and becoming a prominent member of the Los Angles Renaissance the group represented. He has taught, lectured and read his poetry in performance in the major intellectual and urban centers of North America.

Anthony Lyons is a poet and father, currently working on his novel. He is one of the founding members of the Anansi Writers Workshop at The World Stage Gallery in Leimert Park.

YmaSumac Marañón, mother, writer, poet in training, Faith walker, Baha'I and storytellin' bilingual teacher.

Keith Antar Mason is Prince of the Hittite Empire. He lives minutes away from the ocean at night he walks. He sits in coffee houses and writes. In his small kitchen he cooks meals and writes. God fearing, he prays.

Lynn Manning is an award winning poet, playwright, actor, and former World Champion of Blind Judo. His work can be found on his two spoken word releases, "Weights: One blind man's journey," (2005) and "Clarity Of Vision," (1994). To learn more visit: www.lynnmanning.com.

Jose Mendivil was born in California Hospital located in Downtown Los Angeles and raised in Boyle Heights by his Mexican mother and Yaqui/Pima-Papago father. His work has appeared in the Cal State

Northridge Review, Caffeine, LaLa Land, The Red Nations Movement newspaper, Spillway, and The Drumming Between Us.

Sequoia Olivia Mercier, Poet, Mother, Mental Health Counselor, RN has been a member of the Anansi Writers Workshop at The World Stage for twelve years.

Rhonda Mitchell is a poet/writer. Her work has also appeared in the *Mount Voices* anthology. She is a 1999 PEN Emerging Voices fellow and participated in the Voices of Our Nation workshop in San Francisco. She is currently working on her first novel and resides in South Pasadena with her daughter and partner.

Merilene M. Murphy is the author of the freshly published *Under Peace Rising: Poems in English, Spanish & French*, which is available in all major bookstores, at Amazon.Com and at Telepoetics.Com.

Nancy Padron is an LA-based, Afro-Cuban fiction writer, poet, creative writing facilitator, editor, and visual artist. Her work has appeared in 'Dis-Orient Journalizine', the 'Drumming Between Us' and the recently released anthology of fiction, 'Proverbs for the People' (June 2003). Nancy is currently living in Gardena where she is working on her first novel.

E. J. Priestley is a poet, educator and author with three volumes of poetry, including *Abracadabra* and *In The Eagle's Beak*. He has taught at UCLA, USCD and Antioch University.

Jerry Quickley has performed on the PBS documentary series Senior Year and been commissioned to develop a one-man show with the Mark Taper Forum. He is frequently asked to contribute to a variety of books and publications, including Spoken Word Revolution, Twilight of Empire, and many others. Jerry spent time in Iraq before and during the war and occupation, as an un-embedded journalist. He also took hundreds of photos that have proven to be emotionally arresting for their unflinching portrayal of War, The Occupation, and Life in Iraq.

Ariel Robello is a poet based in Echo Park. In 2002, she was awarded an Emerging Voices Rosenthal Fellowship with PEN West. She is the founder of Full Moon Phases, a multi-ethnic, multi-generational women's poetry cipher. Her current joy is teaching poetry in local high schools with PEN in the Classroom and the HeART project. Her first book of poems, "My Sweet Unconditional", was published by Tia Chucha Press.

S. Pearl Sharp is a writer/actress/filmmaker "works words, conjures vision." She wrote *Black Women For Beginners* (non-fiction); 4 volumes of poetry and produced the spoken word CD *On The Sharp Side*. Documentary: *The Healing Passage/Voices From The Water*.

Renee Simms, Former PEN Center USA West Emerging Voice fellow, writes poetry and fiction. She is working towards an MFA in Creative Writing and teaches creative writing at a performing arts high school in Phoenix. Renee misses Lemeirt Park with a fierceness.

Romus Simpson attended the creative writing program at California State University at Long Beach. He is a veteran of more than 360 performances of his poetry in Southern California at various universities, festivals, and other events.

Raaki Solomon has been writing since he was 17 years old, and is now considered an elder. Subject matter covers a wide range, from militant to comedic to love poems, always with a view to enlighten and entertain with depths of expression.

Hannibal Tabu is a journalist, poet, musician and designer living in South Los Angeles. He shouts at infinity from his personal clocktower, www. operative.net.

Jervey Tervalon was born in New Orleans, raised in LA, and now lives in Altadena watching his girls and slowly going nuts. He is author of acclaimed, *Understand This* and most recently, *All the Trouble You Need.*

Imani Tolliver, Poet, visual artist, educator, and community worker, is a graduate of Howard University where she studied English Literature and African-American Studies. She has served as a consultant to community organizations, museums and educators.

Lynne Thompson's work has recently appeared in *Poetry International, Crab Orchard Review, Rattle, PMS* and *Pearl.* Her new chapbook *Through A Window* is forthcoming from Conflux Press in Los Angeles and she will participate in the Poetry in Motion and Newer Poets at the Los Angeles Public Library series during the Poetry Month, 2005.

A. K. Toney is a poet, writer, performance artist; member of the World Stage Anansi Writers Workshop and co-producer of "Resurrection" Wednesday night poetry at the new 5th Street Dick's Coffee House. He has been published numerously in anthologies as well as appeared in national best seller, "Raising Fences-A Blackman's Lovestory" a book of memoirs from Michael Datcher. A. K. has traveled nationally and internationally with the critically acclaimed African American male performance art group known as the Hittite Empire.

Debra A. Varnado lives and writes in Los Angeles. She recently received her MFA in Creative Writing from Antioch University Los Angeles. Her poetry has been published in The Banyan Review and in storySouth. com. In 2003, she received a literary fellowship to attend Summer Poetry in Idyllwild, California.

Pam Ward is a writer, poet, graphic designer and LA native. Her book of poetry is entitled Jacked-Up. She has been published in several anthologies including, "Scream When You Burn," "Catch A Fire," "Calyx," "Men We Cherish," "Grand Passion," and "The Best American Erotica." She is the editor/publisher of "the Supergirl's Handbook." She was the recipient of the California Arts Council Fellowship for Poetry and a New Letters Literary Award. Her first novel, "Want Some Get Some" is seeking a publisher. She is currently working on her second novel, "The Backyard Girl."

Angelo Williams is the Education Policy and Economic Development Consultant to California State Senate Majority Leader Gloria Romero. As the majority leader's education and economic development consultant, Angelo organized the first East Los Angeles economic development summit with State Treasurer Phil Angelides and 24th Senate District Education Summit with Secretary for Education Richard Riordan.

Jaha Zainabu is a God's daughter, a mother, a spoken word and visual artist from Long Beach, Ca. She uses her gifts to enlighten, entertain and educate. Whether to a crowd of five thousand or five, her message is the same, "Let God be God through you."

IX. PERMISSIONS

Shonda Buchanan, "in the time of unforgetting," originally published in *City of Angels*, Vol. 1, No. 1, (Rivendell, Winter 2002). Reprinted with permission of the author.

Wanda Coleman, "Of Cucarachas & Peanut-Peanut Butter: A Poem. For & About Mister Birdsong." Unpublished Copyright for Wanda Coleman 2005; Credit line and copyright information: From Mercurochrome: New Poems, © for Wanda Coleman 2001; reprinted with permission of the author.

Kamau Daáood, "Leimert Park," "Djali," and "Blakey's Sticks" originally published in *The Life of Saxophones: Selected Poems*, (City Lights Publishers, 2005). Reprinted with permission of the author.

K. Curtis Lyle, "Word from Johannesburg," and "Curtis Spiritual Sunwolf: Or the Conversation of Death" originally published in *Electric Church*, (Beyond Baroque Foundation, 2003). Reprinted with permission of the author.

Art Nixon, "Ju-Ju Man (for John Coltrane)," originally published in *Cleveland Anthology* (Parayama Publications, 1975). Reprinted with permission of the author.

Ariel Robello "Ode for the Mic" & "Horizontal geography" originally published in *My Sweet Unconditional* (Tia Chucha Press, 2005). Reprinted with permission of the author.

Romus Simpson, "and they sat there waiting," originally published in *Black Arts Quarterly* (Stanford University, 2005). "on our sixth anniversary," originally published in *X Magazine* (Flipped eye Publishing, London, 2005) as well as in *Black Arts Quarterly* (Stanford University, 2005). Reprinted with permission of the author.

Jaha Zainabu, "Musings" originally published in *The Science of Chocolate Milk Making* (Telepoetics, 2005). Reprinted with permission of the author.

POETS

and if they cannot
save you
they will speak you forever

a child
laughing in the pond
will carry something
of your dreams

sb/nk (Spring 1996)

CPSIA information can be obtained
at www.ICGtesting.com
Printed in the USA
FSOW01n1530310716
23279FS